The GRAMMAR ACE

Instructor's Manual

Written by Duane Bolin
Cover Art by Dave Lilly

 Avyx

8032 S. Grant Way
Littleton, CO 80122
USA

Second Edition

ISBN 978-1-887840-75-0

Avyx, Inc.
8032 South Grant Way
Littleton, CO 80122
USA
303-483-0140
www.avyx.com

Table of Contents

Lessons

Lesson 1: Nouns 1

Lesson 2: Verbs 3

Lesson 3: Sentences 7

Lesson 4: Adjectives 11

Lesson 5: Adverbs, Part 1 15

Lesson 6: Adverbs, Part 2 19

Lesson 7: Pronouns 21

Lesson 8: Direct Objects 25

Lesson 9: Number 27

Lesson 10: Person 31

Lesson 11: Verb Tense 35

Lesson 12: Voice 39

Lesson 13: Synonyms & Antonyms 43

Lesson 14: Predicate Nouns & Adjectives 45

Lesson 15: Prepositions 47

Lesson 16: Indirect Objects 51

Lesson 17: Appositives 53

Lesson 18: Phrases 55

Lesson 19: Clauses 57

Lesson 20: Types of Sentences 61

Lesson 21: Paragraphs 65

Lesson 22: Expository Paragraphs 67

Lesson 23: Persuasive Paragraphs 69

Lesson 24: Descriptive Paragraphs 71

Lesson 25: Narrative Paragraphs 73

Lesson 26: Prefixes & Suffixes 75

Lesson 27: Commas 77

Lesson 28: Analogies 81

Lesson 29: Quotations 83

Lesson 30: Compounds 87

Lesson 31: Contractions 89

Lesson 32: More Nouns 91

Lesson 33: Restrictive & Nonrestrictive Clauses & Phrases 95

Lesson 34: More Pronouns 99

Lesson 35: More Verbs 103

Lesson 36: Gerunds, Participles, & Infinitives 107

Appendices

Appendices 1

Lesson 1: Nouns

> **N**OUN: A noun is the part of speech that names people, places, things, or ideas. Nouns come in three forms. Proper nouns are names; common nouns are the general kinds of things that proper nouns name; pronouns are used in place of proper and common nouns.

Teaching Instruction:

A **noun** is a person, place, or thing. As the most basic of the building blocks of speech, nouns are the first words that most children learn (Mama, Papa, dog, cat).

Ask your children to think of examples of various types of nouns: people (Uncle Gary, brother), places (Denver, city), or things (skateboard, baseball). Children will naturally tend to concentrate on things they can see, feel, hear, and touch. When they're ready, discuss the "invisible" nouns with them. Remind them that the category "things" is very broad, including such "things" as ideas, concepts, or feelings (love, faith, freedom).

Once your children demonstrate a basic understanding of nouns, explain to them that nouns come in three types: proper nouns, common nouns, and pronouns. We will cover pronouns in future lessons. For now, just concentrate on the difference between proper and common nouns. **Proper nouns** are specific names (Seth, Uncle Phil, Indianapolis); **common nouns** are the general kind of thing that proper nouns refer to (boy, man, city).

In A Nutshell:

Noun = person, place, thing, or idea

Proper noun = specific name

Common noun = general kind of thing that a proper noun names

Application:

Choose several activities to do over the course of the week to reinforce what you've taught your children about nouns:

☐ Pull out your **Grammar Rock DVD**[1] and watch **A Noun Is A Person Place Or Thing**.

    ✧ Feel free to watch it multiple times over the course of the week.

    ✧ If your children like to sing, help them memorize the song.

    ✧ Grab the remote and quiz them along the way. Just hit the "pause" button and ask them to name all the nouns they can see on the screen at any particular time.

☐ Have you ever played **I Spy** with your children? If so, you've been practicing nouns with them already. Play variations of the game with your children to help them identify nouns. For example, focus on nouns that begin with the letter "A," then continue with the rest of the alphabet. For a challenge, have your children spot only proper or common nouns.

☐ Go on a **Noun Scavenger Hunt**. Take a walk around your house or yard. Pay close attention to everything you see. You're looking for as many nouns

---

1 **Grammar Rock DVD** refers to the *Schoolhouse Rock!* DVD that is part of the *Grammar Ace* Package.

Notes:

as you can possibly find. What do you see? A book? A table? A tree? These are all nouns. When you're done, write down as many nouns as you can remember on **Side A** of the <u>**Lesson 1: Nouns**</u> Student Activity Sheet. When you're finished, try to classify each noun: Is it a common noun or a proper noun? Did you see your dog Rusty? (proper noun) A toothbrush? (common noun) Circle all of the proper nouns.

☐ Complete the **Noun Matrix** on **Side B** of the <u>**Lesson 1: Nouns**</u> **Student Activity Sheet**. We designed the Noun Matrix to give your children practice with nouns by asking them to focus on people, places, and things with which they're familiar. This matrix can be done independently or as a fun family activity. You can even use it as a guide to review orally throughout the week.

Here is what a completed Noun Matrix might look like:

Category	Common Noun	Proper Noun
A PERSON in your home	sister	Maggie
The PLACE where you live	city	Bainbridge
Your favorite THING	game	Monopoly
A PERSON you'd like to meet	athlete	Peyton Manning
A PLACE you'd like to go	ocean	Atlantic Ocean
A THING you wear	shoe	Rockies baseball hat
A PERSON you saw yesterday	mailman	Rodney
A PLACE you went yesterday	library	Library of Congress
A THING in your house	book	*Johnny Tremain*

Answer Key

Side A: Noun Scavenger Hunt

Answers will vary.

Side B: Noun Matrix

Answers will vary.
Possible answers include:

sister, Julie
house, Jamestown
bike, Spalding volleyball
a senator, President Bush
an island, Virgin Islands
hat, Rockies baseball hat
friend, Samantha
gas station, Diamond Shamrock
blocks, Cuisenaire Rods.

Lesson 2: Verbs

> **V**ERB: Verbs are words that express actions, occurrences, or modes of being. Verbs form the predicate of a sentence and can be inflected for agreement with the subject, for tense, for voice, for mood, or for aspect.

Teaching Instruction:

Verbs are the second main part of speech. While nouns are the things that you talk about, verbs are what you want to say about the nouns. Verbs tell what a noun is or what it does. For example, Ronda runs. What is Ronda? *(proper noun)* What does she do? *(runs) Runs* is a verb.

Verbs can be action verbs or being verbs. Verbs can tell what someone or something did, does, or will do (action verbs) or what it was, is, or will be (being verbs). Don't worry about this distinction at first. Concentrate on action verbs now and come back to being verbs as soon as you're confident your children have a good understanding of action verbs.

When you have an **action verb**, you can form a sentence with just two words. [Note: We'll learn more about sentences in the next lesson.] Here are some examples of two-word sentences featuring action verbs:

> Johnny jumps.
> Ashley cries.
> Karla smiles.

Which words are the nouns? *(Johnny, Ashley, Karla)* Which are the verbs? *(jumps, cries, smiles) Jumps*, *cries*, and *smiles* are all action verbs because they express action. They tell what the nouns do. Ask your children to think of other action verbs for Johnny, Ashley, and Karla. What else do they do? *(talk, laugh, cry, run, etc.)*

Once your children demonstrate an understanding of action verbs, explain to them that verbs can also tell what a noun was, is, or will be. These verbs are called **being verbs** because they express states of being using the verb *to be.* Being verbs usually require at least three words: a noun, a being verb, and one or more words that explain or clarify the noun's state of being.

Here are some examples of simple sentences featuring being verbs:

> Gary is a zookeeper.
> Melinda was sad.
> Amber will be an astronaut.

What are the nouns? *(Gary, Melinda, Amber)* What are the verbs? *(is, was, will be)* What words tell about or clarify the nouns' states of being? *(a zookeeper, sad, an astronaut)* Have your children make up some simple sentences about their current state of being. *(I was hungry. I am tired. I will be happy.)*

Notes:

For your convenience, we have included the following chart that summarizes the proper uses of the verb *to be*. The being verb is underlined and the categories on the right (past perfect, past, past progressive, present, and future) refer to the tense of the verb.

Example	Tense
I <u>had been</u>	
we/you/they <u>had been</u>	Past Perfect (Complete)
he/she/it <u>had been</u>	
I <u>was</u>	
we/you/they <u>were</u>	Past
he/she/it <u>was</u>	
I <u>have been</u>	
we/you/they <u>have been</u>	Past Progressive (Continuing)
he/she/it <u>has been</u>	
I <u>am</u>	
we/you/they <u>are</u>	Present
he/she/it <u>is</u>	
I <u>will be</u>	
we/you/they <u>will be</u>	Future
he/she/it <u>will be</u>	

NOTE: This chart is provided solely as a resource to use with your children. It is not complete and is not intended to be memorized. Instead, use it to spur your children to think of additional sentences featuring being verbs. For example, have your children finish each of the sentences with the correct tense of the verb *to be* from the chart.

Yesterday, she…*(was)*
Today, they………*(are)*
Tommorow, we …*(will be)*

In A Nutshell:

Verbs tell what a noun is or what it does.

Action verbs tell what someone or something did, does, or will do.

Being verbs tell what someone or something was, is, or will be.

Application:

Choose several activities to do over the course of the week to reinforce what you've taught your children about verbs:

☐ Watch **Verb: That's What's Happening** on your **Grammar Rock** DVD.

   ✧   Watch it once a day until your children fully understand verbs.

   ✧   If your children like to sing, help them memorize the song.

   ✧   Ask your children to identify action and being verbs they can see on the screen at different times.

☐ Play **I Spy** with your children again. Use the opportunity to review nouns first, and then add a new dimension to the game. For each noun that your children identify, ask them to supply an appropriate verb to go with each noun. For a challenge, have your children spot only action or being verbs.

☐ Do some **Verb Chores**. Think of verbs that you can do around the house (dust, mop, vacuum, clean, tidy, etc.) and then do them! You'll be learning about verbs and making your mom very happy at the same time.

☐ Play **Verb Charades**. You will need at least two people for this game. Write 10-20 different verbs on small slips of paper and put them in a hat or other container. Have one player select a verb from the hat and then act out that verb. The other players have to guess what verb is being acted out. If you have several players, form teams and keep score. If you need some help getting started, here are some possible verbs you could use: jump, dance, swim, row, sing, sleep, write, cry, laugh, stir, etc.

☐ Create some **Silly Sentences** by filling in the blanks on **Side A** of the **Lesson 2: Verbs** **Student Activity Sheet**. If the blank needs a noun, write in a noun. If it needs a verb, write in a verb. Make your sentences as silly as possible! When you're finished, try to classify each verb: Is it an action verb or a being verb? Write an "A" above all the action verbs and a "B" above all the being verbs.

☐ Complete the **Name That Verb** chart on **Side B** of the **Lesson 2: Verbs** **Student Activity Sheet**. For each verb listed in the left column, identify whether it is an action verb or a being verb, and then place a check mark in the appropriate column.

Answer Key

Side A: Silly Sentences

Answers will vary.

Side B: Name That Verb

Action: *jogs; swam; hunted; writes; grins, exploded*

Being: *am; was; had been, will be*

Lesson 3: Sentences

> **S**ENTENCE: A sentence is a grammatical unit of one or more words expressing a complete thought or idea, such as an assertion, a question, a command, a wish, an exclamation, or the performance of an action. Sentences begin with a capital letter and end with proper punctuation.

Teaching Instruction:

In your first two lessons, you learned about the two most basic building blocks of sentences: nouns and verbs. Armed with that knowledge, this lesson on sentences should be a breeze!

A **sentence** is a group of words that (1) has a noun (called the subject), (2) a verb (called the predicate), and (3) expresses a complete thought. The **subject** is who or what the sentence is about. The **predicate** tells you about the subject: what the subject did, what happened to it, or what it "is."

The shortest sentence normally consists of two words: one noun and one verb. (See the ***Just for Fun!*** section below for the exception to this rule!) Don't forget: the verb in a two-word sentence will almost always be an action verb. Here are some examples of some two-word sentences:

> Marcus snores.
> Fay stares.
> Wayne frowns.
> Gary laughs.

Can you name the nouns? (*Marcus, Fay, Wayne, Gary*) What about the verbs? (*snores, stares, frowns, laughs*)

If a group of words is missing a subject or a predicate or does not form a complete thought, it is called a **sentence fragment**. Here are a couple of examples of sentence fragments. Can you identify what is wrong with each?

> The dog with the black spots.
> When the penguins saw the popcorn maker.
> Running and jumping like wild.

The dog with the black spots is missing a verb. What is the dog doing? *When the penguins saw the popcorn maker* is an incomplete thought. What did they do when they saw the popcorn maker? *Running and jumping like wild* needs a noun. Who or what was running and jumping like wild? My guess? I'll bet the penguins were the ones running and jumping like wild when they saw the popcorn maker. Or, then again, maybe it was the dog with the black spots…

There are two other very important rules about sentences that you need to learn and never, ever forget:

1. Every sentence should always begin with a **capital letter**.

2. Every sentence should always end with a closing **punctuation mark**: a period (.), a question mark (?), or an exclamation point (!).

The **period** (.) is used at the end of a sentence that makes a statement, request, or mild command. For example:

> The aardvark is Phil's favorite animal.
> Hand me the fruitcake, please.
> Bolinville is a fun place to visit.

Notes:

The **question mark** (?) is used at the end of a sentence that asks a direct question. For example:

Where is my armadillo?
Why did you put your cat in my garage?
When will Mr. Whelan fix my computer?

The **exclamation point** (!) is used at the end of an interjection or exclamatory sentence. It communicates strong emotion or surprise. For example:

I don't believe it!
My possum is missing!
You're kidding!

Capital letters and punctuation marks act like traffic signals. When you put several sentences together, proper capitalization and punctuation allow you to know when sentences begin and when they end. This helps you to read them in the proper way.

In A Nutshell:

Sentence = noun + verb + complete thought

Subject = who or what the sentence is about

Predicate = what the subject did, what happened to it, or what it "is"

Every sentence should start with a capital letter and end with the proper punctuation mark: a period (statements or mild commands), a question mark (questions), or an exclamation point (to show strong emotion).

Just for Fun!

Did you notice the definition of sentence at the beginning of the lesson? A sentence is a grammatical unit of one or more words…*One word? A sentence can be only one word?* You bet it can!

Go!
Run!
Stop!

These are all examples of one-word sentences. *But I thought a sentence had to have both a noun and a verb? Go, run, and stop are all verbs. Where are the nouns?* Well, these sentences are the exception to the general rule, but they do have a subject. It's the same subject for each sentence. Can you guess what it is? It's…you!

These sentences have **implied** or **understood subjects**. When you run across them, you will be able to tell from the context (the sentences that come before and after) who or what the subject of the sentence is. You will often find implied or understood subjects in sentences expressing a command. For example:

Go to your room.
Take out the trash.
Give me that!

As you can see, sentences with implied or understood subjects can be more than one word, but they still lack a noun as the subject in the sentence. The implied subject is understood by the reader from the context, even though it is not stated.

As long as we're talking about implied or understood subjects, we might as well mention that there are also **implied** or **understood predicates**. For example:

> Pam asked, "Would you please bring me some green beans?"
> "I might," Michael replied.

We know what Michael means, but his sentence does not include the complete predicate: "I might *bring you some green beans*." The predicate is implied or understood.

Application:

Choose several activities to do over the course of the week to reinforce what you've taught your children about sentences:

☐ Pop your **Grammar Rock** DVD into your DVD player and review **A Noun is A Person Place Or Thing** and **Verb: That's What's Happening**. Then watch **The Tale Of Mr. Morton** to learn more about subjects and predicates.

   ✧ Reviewing each of the songs throughout the week will help your children see how nouns and verbs naturally work together within a sentence.

   ✧ As always, help your children memorize the songs if they like to sing.

   ✧ Apply what you've learned about sentences, subjects, and predicates to the noun and verb songs. For example, ask your children to identify the subjects and predicates in the sentences used in the noun and verb songs.

☐ If your children enjoyed playing **I Spy** with nouns and verbs, then by all means continue with sentences. Review nouns first. Then have your children identify verbs that go with each noun. Finally, ask your children to form basic sentences with the nouns and verbs they've spotted.

☐ Make a set of punctuation flashcards. Using three 3"x5" cards, write the punctuation marks on them (period, question mark, and exclamation point). Then play **End That Sentence!** Make up some silly sentences and then say them to your children. When you're done saying each sentence, have your children hold up the flashcard with the proper punctuation for the sentence. Be sure to incorporate a mixture of sentences that end in each of the punctuation marks. When you think your children have mastered this game, switch roles. See if they can make up sentences on their own for you to guess the proper ending punctuation.

☐ Play **What's Wrong With These Sentences?** on **Side A** of the **Lesson 3: Sentences Student Activity Sheet**. Look carefully at each of the sentences and try to identify what is wrong with each one. Note: Some sentences may have more than one thing wrong with them. Put three lines under a letter if it needs to be capitalized. Insert the proper punctuation mark if it's missing and draw a small arrow pointing to it. For a challenge, underline the nouns that are subjects and circle the verbs that are predicates. Be careful! Two of the sentences are not even sentences at all. Can you find the two sentence fragments and add what's missing to make them real sentences?

☐ Write six crazy **Imagination Sentences** on **Side B** of the **Lesson 3: Sentences** Student Activity Sheet. Choose a noun from the subject column and a verb from the predicate column, and then write a sentence with those words. Use each of the punctuation marks (periods, question marks, and exclamation points) at least twice. When you're done, keep your sheet to use in future lessons.

Answer Key

Side A: What's Wrong With These Sentences?

Answers will vary.
Possible answers include:

1. The <u>armadillo</u> drove the car to the store.←

2. A <u>mouse</u> (ran) up the tree.

3. **Fragment.** *Possible:* The twelve <u>kangaroos</u> with the purple bow ties (hopped) *over the hill.*

4. (Did) <u>Fred</u> (feed) the rabbit?←

5. **Fragment.** *Possible:* <u>Jake</u> (swam) in the lake all day long.

6. The chicken <u>coop</u> (is) on fire! ←

7. <u>Why</u> (is) the <u>moose</u> (eating) a banana?

8. Five <u>geese</u> (were playing) cards.←

Side B: Imagination Sentences

Answers will vary.

Lesson 4: Adjectives

> A DJECTIVE: Adjectives are words that modify a noun, usually to describe a quality of something named, to indicate its quantity or extent, or to distinguish a thing from something else.

Teaching Instruction:

In the last lesson, you learned to create basic sentences. In this lesson, you're going to learn how to make those sentences more interesting by adding adjectives.

Adjectives are words that describe nouns. For example:

Happy children smile.
Angry dogs bark.
Hot people enjoy *cold* sodas.

Adjectives make your writing more interesting by adding to the reader's understanding of the nouns you use. For example, let's say you're writing to your friend whose mom trains monkeys. You might write:

Your mom trains monkeys.

This sentence already contains one adjective. What is it? (*your*) *Your* tells the reader which mom you're talking about. Now, it's already kind of interesting that you have a friend whose mom trains monkeys. But it could be even more interesting if you add some more adjectives. Take a look at these sentences and see if you can identify the adjectives.

Your mom trains seven monkeys.
Your mom trains seven mean monkeys.
Your mom trains seven mean, fat monkeys.
Your brave mom trains seven mean, fat monkeys.

What do you think? These sentences are definitely more interesting! What adjectives did you identify? (*Your, seven, mean, fat, brave*) Did you notice that you can describe a noun with more than one adjective by stringing the adjectives together? Try it yourself now.

Take the noun *giraffe* and try to think of as many adjectives as you can to describe it. Then make up a sentence using those adjectives. String several together to make a really interesting sentence! Here is an example:

Adjectives: tall, yellow, old, hungry, sad
Sentence: The tall, old, yellow giraffe was sad and hungry.

As soon as your children have a basic understanding of adjectives, explain that some words—like *seven* and *mean*—are always and only adjectives. Other words—like *fat* and *Your*—can serve as adjectives but are nouns (fat) and pronouns (Your) too. Even verbs can serve as adjectives: a *crumpled* sheet of paper. Just remember to see how the word is being used in the sentence. If it's describing a noun, then it's functioning as an adjective.

Finally, have your children memorize the three special adjectives (*a, an*, and *the*) called **articles**. Articles are adjectives because they help the reader understand which specific thing is being discussed. For example:

The dogs dance.
A tractor rumbles.
An egg breaks.

In A Nutshell:

Adjectives describe nouns.

A, an, and *the* are special adjectives called **articles**.

Just for Fun!

Adjectives come in one of three forms: **positive**, **comparative**, or **superlative**.

The **positive form** describes a word without comparing it to anything else. For example:

> That badger is mean.

The **comparative form** describes a word by comparing it to one other thing. Comparative adjectives often use the ending *-er* or the words *more* or *less*. For example:

> That badger is meaner than the hedgehog.

The **superlative form** describes a word by comparing it to two or more other things. Superlative adjectives often use the ending *-est* or the words *most* or *least*. For example:

> That badger is the meanest varmint in these woods.

Application:

Choose several activities to do over the course of the week to reinforce what you've taught your children about adjectives:

☐ Watch **Unpack Your Adjectives** on your **Grammar Rock** DVD.

    ✧ You should also feel free to continue to review the songs covered already: **A Noun is A Person Place Or Thing**, **Verb: That's What's Happening**, and **The Tale Of Mr. Morton**.

☐ While you're driving in the car with your children, play adjective **I Spy.** Have someone be the "spy" and the others have to guess what noun was spied based upon the list of adjectives the "spy" uses to describe it.

☐ Play **The Doctor's Cat.** Take turns thinking of things that describe the doctor's cat. At each turn repeat all the adjectives and add one. For example, here is how a game might begin: "The doctor's cat is a fluffy cat." "The doctor's cat is a fluffy, fat cat." "The doctor's cat is a fluffy, fat, wet cat." Etc. For fun variations, make all adjectives start with the same letter. Or, use alphabetical order for each adjective to help you recall the list with more ease.

☐ As all psychiatrists know, a game of **Word Association** can be just what the doctor ordered. So here's your chance to psychoanalyze your children in the guise of a fun grammar game. Note: Couch is optional. You say a noun and have your children respond—as quickly as possible—with the first adjective that comes to mind. For example: you say "frog"; they say "green." Have fun and, if you're brave enough, switch places and let them analyze you!

☐ Play **Madjectives!** on **Side A** of the <u>**Lesson 4: Adjectives**</u> **Student Activity Sheet**. Without reading the paragraph first, ask your children to create a list of 15 colorful adjectives. Ask them to be as creative as possible. Instead of *big* and *ugly*, use words like *gigantic* and *hideous*. When they're done, fill in the blanks in the paragraph with the adjectives on your children's list. Then read the paragraph out loud to see how silly and fun adjectives can be...and how important it is to choose adjectives wisely! You can play this game over and over again—just keep thinking up new lists of adjectives.

☐ Using your **Imagination Sentences** from **Side B** of the <u>**Lesson 3: Sentences**</u> **Student Activity Sheet**, rewrite each of those sentences on **Side B** of the <u>**Lesson 4: Adjectives**</u> **Student Activity Sheet**, expanding each sentence by adding some fun adjectives. Each sentence should include either one adjective *other than* an article or one adjective *plus* an article. Use different adjectives in every sentence. Keep your finished paper for use in later lessons.

Answer Key

Side A: Madjectives!

Answers will vary.

Side B: Expanded Imagination Sentences

Answers will vary.

Notes:

Lesson 5: Adverbs, Part 1

> ADVERB: Adverbs are words that usually modify verbs, adjectives, other adverbs, prepositions, phrases, clauses, or sentences. They typically express some relation of manner or quality, place, time, degree, number, cause, opposition, affirmation, or denial.

Teaching Instruction:

Building upon the last lesson about adjectives, we will now look at another kind of word that can make sentences more exciting. **Adverbs** add to our understanding of verbs. Adverbs tell us how, when, or where the verb happened (or is happening or will yet happen). For example, consider these sentences:

> The alligators swam.
> Grandma Loretta yelled.
> The mourners wept.

These sentences convey some basic meaning and are slightly interesting, but couldn't they be better? Now compare them to these sentences with adverbs (in *italics*):

> The alligators swam *yesterday*.
> Grandma Loretta yelled *loudly*.
> The mourners wept *uncontrollably*.

What do you think? Wouldn't you rather read the sentences with the adverbs? **Important Note:** If you find a word that ends in *-ly*, it is probably an adverb!

When you begin writing with adverbs, remember that you can place adverbs in various places: right in front of the verbs they describe, right behind the verbs they describe, or even some distance away from their verbs. For example, consider the placement of the adverb *quickly* in the following sentences:

> Nemo *quickly* jumped on the sea horse.
> Nemo jumped *quickly* onto the sea horse.
> *Quickly*, the small fish jumped onto the sea horse.
> Nemo jumped onto the galloping sea horse *quickly*—before it
> got away.

Adverbs open up a whole world of expression and add power to your writing. They can make the most basic prose more interesting and fun. Use them often.

In A Nutshell:

Adverbs describe verbs.
If you find a word that ends in **-ly**, it is probably an adverb!

Just for Fun!

Like adjectives, adverbs also come in three forms: positive, comparative, or superlative. The **positive form** describes a verb without comparing it to anything else. For example:

> My favorite cow, Buttercup, walks gracefully.

The **comparative form** describes a word by comparing it to one other thing. Comparative adverbs often use the ending *-er* or the words *more* or *less*. For example:

> Buttercup walks more gracefully than her sister, Teapot.

The **superlative form** describes a word by comparing it to two or more other things. Superlative adjectives often use the ending *-est* or the words *most* or *least*. For example:

> Of all the cows at Green Acres, Teapot walks most clumsily.

Application:

Choose several activities to do over the course of the week to reinforce what you've taught your children about adverbs:

☐ Watch **Lolly, Lolly, Lolly, Get Your Adverbs Here** on your **Grammar Rock DVD.**

✦ You should also feel free to continue to review the songs covered already: **A Noun is A Person Place Or Thing, Verb: That's What's Happening, The Tale Of Mr. Morton,** and **Unpack Your Adjectives.**

☐ Play a fun game of **Back and Forth** to form silly sentences with adverbs. You'll need two or more players to work together to make short adverb sentences, according to the following rules:

Player 1:	states an article (A/An/The)
Player 2:	provides a noun
Player 1 (or 3):	adds a verb
Player 2 (or 4):	adds an adverb that describes the verb
Player 1 (or 5):	completes the sentence

Here's how a sample round might go:

Player 1:	"The…
Player 2:	"…aardvark…"
Player 1:	"…jumped…"
Player 2:	"…mightily…"
Player 1:	"…onto the passing freight train."

See how creative, fun and sometimes crazy the sentences become!

☐ Play **Word Association** using adverbs. You say a verb and have your children respond—as quickly as possible—with the first adverb that comes to mind. For example: you say "destroys"; they say "completely." Don't forget to switch places and let them challenge you!

☐ Practice creating **L-Y** adverbs on **Side A** of the <u>**Lesson 5: Adverbs, Part 1**</u> **Student Activity Sheet.** Correctly add the *-ly* ending to the words provided to complete the sentences. Spelling is important! Feel free to make up additional words and sentences if your children enjoy this exercise.

☐ Using your **Expanded Imagination Sentences** from **Side B** of the **Lesson 4: Adjectives** Student Activity Sheet, rewrite each of those sentences on **Side B** of the **Lesson 5: Adverbs, Part 1** Student Activity Sheet, expanding each sentence further by adding a creative adverb. Use different adverbs in every sentence. Keep your activity sheet for use in later lessons.

Answer Key

Side A: L-Y

1. gracefully
2. smoothly
3. attentively
4. fluently
5. beautifully
6. gleefully
7. poorly
8. immediately
9. terribly
10. quickly
11. sparingly
12. madly
13. wistfully
14. happily
15. deftly
16. winsomely

Side B: Expanded (Even Further) Imagination Sentences

Answers will vary.

Notes:

Lesson 6: Adverbs, Part 2

> $\mathbb{A}$DVERB: Adverbs are words that usually modify verbs, adjectives, other adverbs, prepositions, phrases, clauses, or sentences. They typically express some relation of manner or quality, place, time, degree, number, cause, opposition, affirmation, or denial.

Teaching Instruction:

In the last lesson, we learned that adverbs modify verbs. That's not all adverbs can do, though. **Adverbs** also can describe or modify our understanding of an adjective or another adverb. For example:

Powder blue flowers grew by the side of the road.

Blue describes the color of the flowers. Therefore, *blue* is an adjective. What color blue were the flowers, though? Dark, midnight blue? Royal blue? No, they were *powder* blue. *Powder* describes the adjective *blue*, so *powder* is an adverb. Here's another example:

The antelope ran extremely quickly.

Quickly is an adverb because it describes how the antelope ran. *Extremely* describes the adverb *quickly*, so it is an adverb too. Can you spot all of the adverbs in the following sentences?

The girl in the light green dress sang so beautifully.
The very bright light of the stage seems to be her natural habitat.

In the first sentence, the adverbs are *light, so*, and *beautifully*. *Light* is an adverb because it describes the adjective *green*. *Beautifully* is an adverb because it describes the verb *sang*. So is also an adverb because it modifies the adverb *beautifully*. In the second sentence, the only adverb is *very*, which modifies the adjective *bright*.

In A Nutshell:

Adverbs also can describe or modify our understanding of an adjective or another adverb.

Application:

Choose several activities to do over the course of the week to reinforce what you've taught your children about adverbs:

☐ Watch **Lolly, Lolly, Lolly, Get Your Adverbs Here** on your **Grammar Rock DVD** again.

❖ Continue to review the songs covered already as well: **A Noun is A Person Place Or Thing**, **Verb: That's What's Happening**, **The Tale Of Mr. Morton**, and **Unpack Your Adjectives**.

☐ Play a rousing game of **Funny Monkey**. Starting with the sentence "The funny monkey ran," take turns adding new adverbs to the sentence. For example, "The *very* funny monkey ran." "The *very* funny monkey ran *slowly*." "The *very* funny monkey ran *rather slowly*." See how many adverbs you are able to add (and remember!) and still have an understandable sentence. When you're done, start with a new sentence and keep going. Try "The funny monkey laughed…." or "The funny monkey swung…."

☐ Review your **Expanded (Even Further) Imagination Sentences** from **Side B** of the <u>**Lesson 5: Adverbs, Part 1**</u> **Student Activity Sheet**. Can you add any more adverbs to them? Look at each of the adjectives and adverbs you've already used to see if they can be modified even further with additional adverbs.

☐ Help your children play **Adverb Charades**. Have one child volunteer to leave the room while the other players choose an adverb, such as "loudly." When the volunteer returns, he must guess the adverb by asking the other players to do things "that way." For example, he might ask one of the other players to "talk that way." The other player would then talk loudly. As soon as he guesses the adverb correctly (or gives up), ask for the next volunteer. If you can't do what you're asked (for example, if asked to sit loudly), you should just say, "I don't want to," but say it in such a way as to provide a clue to the adverb (i.e., say "I don't want to" loudly).

☐ Compare **Adjective and Adverb Forms** by completing the sentences on **Side A** of the <u>**Lesson 6: Adverbs, Part 2**</u> **Student Activity Sheet**. Each set of sentences will use either an adjective or adverb form of a word. Fill in the blank with the other form. This exercise will help your children learn the differences (and similarities) between adjectives and adverbs.

☐ Play **Madverbs!** on **Side B** of the <u>**Lesson 6: Adverbs, Part 2**</u> **Student Activity Sheet**. Without reading the paragraph first, ask your children to create a list of 15 creative adverbs. When they're done, fill in the blanks in the paragraph with the adverbs on your children's list. Then read the paragraph out loud to see how silly and fun adverbs can be! You can play this game over and over again—just keep thinking up new lists of adverbs.

Answer Key

Side A: Adjective and Adverb Forms

1. smoothly
2. terrible
3. warmly
4. desperately
5. swimming
6. cold
7. happily
8. brusque
9. sad
10. cheaply
11. sly
12. angrily
13. sheepishly
14. lazily
15. excited

Side B: Madverbs!

Answers will vary.

Lesson 7: Pronouns

> **P**RONOUN: Pronouns are words that are used as substitutes for nouns and whose referents are named or understood from the surrounding context.

Teaching Instruction:

In this lesson, we return to nouns again. Instead of common nouns and proper nouns, though, we will discuss the third type of noun. **Pronouns** are words used in place of common and proper nouns. In other words, pronouns are words that "stand in the place of" common or proper nouns once people know what you're talking about. For example:

> Duane kicked the ball. *He* kicked *it* into the net.
> Karleen tripped over the toys. *She* didn't see *them* on the floor.
> The spaceship hovered over Henrietta. *It* was waiting for *her.*

Do you see how *He* replaces *Duane*, *it* replaces *ball*, *She* replaces *Karleen*, *them* replaces *toys*, *It* replaces *spaceship*, and *her* replaces *Henrietta*? Given the first sentence in each pair, it's easy for the reader to understand what nouns the pronouns are referring to. But what about the following sentence?

> They ran over it with the lawn mower.

You're probably asking yourself, "Who is *They*?" and "What is *it*?" Those are both great questions, because we don't know! Without the proper context, we don't know what nouns these pronouns refer to. They're missing their antecedents.

Antecedent is the fancy word that means "the noun that the pronoun refers to or takes the place of." Every pronoun must have a clear antecedent. Otherwise your writing will be confusing and difficult to read. For example, try to read the following paragraph:

> Beth and Karla were standing in the kitchen looking for the dogs. She was ready to go to work, but Beth couldn't find her keys. "I thought I heard them a minute ago," said Karla.

Confusing? Absolutely. Who is ready to go to work? Beth or Karla? Whose keys are lost? What did Karla hear? The keys or the dogs? This paragraph does not clearly identify the antecedents of the pronouns. As a result, it is difficult to read and understand. Here's an important rule to remember when you write:

Never use a pronoun unless you know that its antecedent is obvious.

Set forth below is a long list of pronouns. Don't make your children memorize this list. It is not comprehensive and should not be used for testing purposes. We provide it only as a resource for your children to consult as they study pronouns.

Common Pronouns					
all	any	anybody	anyone	anything	both
each	either	everybody	everyone	everything	few
he	her	herself	him	himself	his
I	it	its	itself	little	many
me	mine	more	most	much	myself
neither	nobody	none	nothing	one	other
others	ours	ourselves	she	some	somebody
someone	something	that	theirs	them	themselves
these	they	this	those	us	we
what	whatever	which	whichever	who	whoever
whom	whomever	whose	you	yours	yourself

As you can see, there are many, many different types of pronouns with many, many rules that govern their proper usage. However, for now, just concentrate on the basics. We'll learn more about specific types of pronouns and special rules in later lessons.

In A Nutshell:

Pronouns are words that "stand in the place of" common or proper nouns once people know what you're talking about.

An **antecedent** is the noun that a pronoun refers to or takes the place of. Never use a pronoun unless you know that its antecedent is obvious!

Application:

Choose several activities to do over the course of the week to reinforce what you've taught your children about pronouns:

☐ Watch **Rufus Xavier Sarsaparilla** on your **Grammar Rock** DVD. If you want, review **A Noun is A Person Place Or Thing** as well.

☐ Play **Pronoun Concentration**. Get some index cards. Any even number of cards will work, but the more you can use, the more fun the game will be.

Divide the cards into two piles. On half of the cards, write a noun. Make sure to use a combination of various nouns: singular, plural, male, female, and neutral. Here are some examples of nouns you could use: boy, girls, John, Jane, boat, trees, sisters, brother, car, trains, women, man, pig, sheep, signs, mailbox, etc. Then, on the other half of the cards, write a pronoun. Again, make sure to use a similar variety of pronouns. For examples of pronouns you could use, please refer to the list on the previous page. When you're done, lay all the cards face down. Take turns picking up pairs of cards. If the pair you pick up would work as a pronoun-antecedent pair (for example, "bat" and "it"), you get to keep the cards in your pile. If not (for example, "Fred" and "she"), you need to turn them back over. The person with the most cards in his pile when all cards have been used is the winner!

☐ Play **A Penny For A Pronoun** throughout the day. Get a bag full of pennies and keep it in your pocket. Explain to your children that you will give them a penny every time you use a pronoun and they catch you. Purposefully try to use more common and proper nouns rather than pronouns. Even refer to yourself in the third person for fun (for example, "Judy loves ice cream" rather than "I love ice cream"). Once you're out of pennies, turn the tables and make your children pay you a penny every time you catch them using a pronoun. For a fun variation, play a "high stakes" game in which you pick out certain, infrequently-used pronouns, such as whom, whichever, itself, whatever, whoever, etc. Pay a quarter each time you're caught using them.

☐ Complete the **Pronoun-Antecedent Match** lesson on **Side A** of the **Lesson 7: Pronouns Student Activity Sheet**. Match each pronoun on the left side of the page with the appropriate noun(s) on the right side of the page. Draw a line between the appropriate pronoun-antecedent pairs.

☐ Practice **Using Pronouns** by completing the exercise on **Side B** of the **Lesson 7: Pronouns Student Activity Sheet**. Rewrite the sentences and replace the underlined noun(s) with the correct pronoun(s).

Answer Key

Side A: Pronoun-Antecedent Match

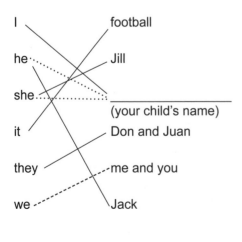

I
he
she
it
they
we

football
Jill
_____
(your child's name)
Don and Juan
me and you
Jack

······ *Indicates a possible answer.*

Side B: Using Pronouns

1. He swam quickly.
2. Yesterday, he took her shirt to the cleaners.
3. It glows brightly at midnight.
4. This afternoon, he will wax it.
5. Did either work yesterday?
6. He has to plow it tomorrow.
7. It is her favorite holiday.
8. She couldn't believe he didn't drop it.

Notes:

Lesson 8: Direct Objects

> **D**IRECT OBJECT: A direct object is a word or phrase expressing the result of the action of a verb.

Teaching Instruction:

In this lesson, we're going to take a look at yet another function of the multi-faceted noun. You've already learned that nouns often function as the subject of a sentence. When a noun acts as a subject, it performs the action in a sentence. A noun can be a direct object, too. A **direct object** receives the action directly from the subject or is directly affected by the action. For example:

The truck hit the pothole.

What are the two nouns? *(truck, pothole)* Which noun is the subject, i.e., which noun does the acting? *(truck)* Which noun is the direct object, i.e., which noun receives the action? *(pothole)* Here are a few more examples:

Maggie cooked a burrito.
Seth created a pizza.
They ate dinner together.

What are the subjects? *(Maggie, Seth, They)* What are the direct objects? *(burrito, pizza, dinner)*

In A Nutshell:

Direct Objects are nouns that receive the action directly from the subject or are directly affected by the action.

Just For Fun!

An **object complement** is a noun, pronoun, or adjective that follows a direct object and renames it or tells what the direct object has become. For example:

Amber and Ronda painted the town *red*.
The residents of Westminster elected Gary *mayor*.

Application:

Choose several activities to do over the course of the week to reinforce what you've taught your children about direct objects:

☐ Review any or all of the songs on your **Grammar Rock** DVD that we've covered thus far.

☐ Play a rousing game of **The Awful Aardvark.** Make up some sentences about what the awful aardvark might do, and then have your children finish the sentence with a creative direct object. For example, if you say, "The awful aardvark tripped," then your children might say, "the kangaroo." Other verbs you can try: smacked, jumped, attacked, yelled, fell, pushed, pulled, etc. Feel free to make up your own creative verbs. For a variation, challenge your children to add colorful adjectives and adverbs as well.

□ Challenge your children to become **Newspaper Sleuths**. Browse through a local newspaper to find a few child-friendly articles. Then ask your children to read the articles and circle as many direct objects as they can find. If that's too easy for them, ask them to find subjects, verbs, adjectives, and/or adverbs too.

□ **Pick and Choose** subjects, verbs, and direct objects from the chart on **Side A** of the <u>Lesson 8: Direct Objects</u> **Student Activity Sheet**, and then use them to create five crazy sentences. Note: You can mix and match the subjects, verbs, and direct objects however you like. You do not have to put together sentences using all the words in any particular row. You do, however, need to make sure that you use each word no more than once. Have fun!

□ Complete the **Label That Sentence** exercise on **Side B** of the <u>Lesson 8: Direct Objects</u> **Student Activity Sheet**. Each of the sentences listed contains a subject and a direct object. Label each subject with an "S" and each direct object with a "DO." For a challenge, label any verbs with "V," any adjectives with "ADJ," and any adverbs with "ADV."

Answer Key

Side A: Pick and Choose

Answers will vary.

Side B: Label That Sentence

   adj   adj   s   v   adj   do
1. The hungry bear stalked its prey.

   adj s   v   adj   do   adv
2. A boy threw a boomerang swiftly.

   adj   adj   s   v   adj adj   do
3. The garbage truck dumped the stinky trash.

   adj   s   v   adj do
4. Two tornadoes leveled the town.

   adj   s   v   adj adj   do
5. The hunter spied the brown deer.

      s   v   adj   do   adv
6. Consuela roasted her marshmallow slowly.

   adj   s   v   adj   do
7. The bookmobile held thirty books.

   adj   adj   s   v   adj   do
8. An angry beaver defended his dam.

Lesson 9: Number

> $\mathcal{N}$UMBER: Number refers to the distinction of word form to denote reference to one or more than one.

Teaching Instruction:

Number refers to the grammatical concept of whether there is one or more than one of something. **Singular** means there is one of something. **Plural** means there is more than one of something. OK, you're probably thinking, "No problem! I understand this. One. Or more than one. Got it!" Wait just a second, though. Fancy verbiage aside, the grammar concept of number does get a little more complicated than just counting.

All nouns have a number: they are either singular (one) or plural (more than one). Usually, plurals are formed by adding s to the singular version of a noun. However, there are many exceptions to this rule. For example, here are some sentences that show the many differences between singular and plural forms of nouns:

I need a *dish*! The *dishes* are over there.

Mr. Meyers has one *dog*. We have three *dogs*.

My name is *Abby*. There are three *Abbys* in my class.

I love my *wife*. The *wives* of pastors must be very patient people.

This *donkey* won't move. Well, *donkeys* are known for being stubborn.

My *roof* is leaking. After the hurricane, all the *roofs* in town are leaking.

My teacher gave us a *quiz* today. She has given us three *quizzes* this week!

I love my pet *goose*. He stays with me even when all the other *geese* fly south.

Sarah grabbed one *tomato*. Old Man Jenkins stuffed four *tomatoes* into his bag.

Waiter! There's a *fly* in my soup! Get over it. There are *flies* everywhere in here.

John has a *child* named Amy. Jason has three *children* named Ed, Fred, and Ned.

My *brother-in-law* used to live in a yurt. You can never have too many *brothers-in-law*.

As you can see, there are many exceptions to the general rule of creating a plural noun by adding *s* to the singular version. Use the examples above as a guide, but always consult a dictionary if you are unsure of the proper spelling of the plural form of a noun.

Verbs also have singular and plural forms. If you have a singular subject, then its verb must be singular. If the subject is plural, then its verb must be plural. This rule is called **subject-verb agreement**. For example:

Correct:	Incorrect:
Jack runs.	Jack run.
The boys run.	The boys runs.

Notes:

Hopefully, subject-verb agreement will seem somewhat intuitive. Based upon your experiences with speech, you will likely be able to "hear" whether the subject and verb agree. If they don't, the sentence won't sound "right."

There are two instances, however, that can be tricky: (1) **collective nouns**; and (2) when a proper name includes a plural noun. In both of these situations, it can be difficult to keep the numbers of nouns straight. In both cases, though, the rule is the same: You should use singular verbs with both collective nouns and proper names that include a plural noun. If it helps, you can think of these special cases as **singular plurals**!

For example, the word *family* is a collective noun; it groups a large number of individuals into one entity. Following the rule, you should use a singular verb with family:

Correct:	Incorrect:
My family *includes* three people.	My family *include* three people.

Can you hear the difference between the correct and incorrect versions? If you prefer to use a plural verb with a collective noun, then you must speak of the members of the collective noun. For example:

The family *members* include a father, a mother, and a son.

In the second instance—when a proper name includes a plural noun—remember that the entire name is a proper noun and should therefore use the singular form of the verb. For example:

Correct:	Incorrect:
The Masters *is* the best tournament.	The Masters *are* the best tournament.

Be careful! You can't rely on your ear as much when it comes to proper names that include a plural noun. The plural noun can be deceiving, leading you to think a plural verb is needed when, in reality, a singular noun is correct. Here's another example:

Correct:	Incorrect:
Rugrats is on at noon.	*Rugrats are* on at noon.

In A Nutshell:

Number = whether there is one or more than one of something

Singular = one of something

Plural = more than one of something

Subject-verb agreement = singular subjects require singular verbs; plural subjects require plural verbs. Use singular verbs with both collective nouns and proper names that include a plural noun.

Application:

Choose several activities to do over the course of the week to reinforce what you've taught your children about the number of nouns and verbs and subject-verb agreement:

☐ Review ***A Noun is A Person Place Or Thing***, ***Verb: That's What's Happening,*** and ***The Tale Of Mr. Morton*** on your ***Grammar Rock*** **DVD**.

☐ As the lesson pointed out, it is often easy to "hear" whether a sentence's subject and verb agree as they're supposed to. Help your children **Develop an Ear** for subject-verb agreement by practicing sentences with them orally. For example, make up some sentences about playing or hunting or skydiving or whatever. Talk about a single person doing the activity and then a bunch of people doing it. Try using the same verbs with *single* and *plural* subjects. Try them with the subject *I* and then with the subject *we*, or compare *he* to *them* or *she* to *we*…. Encourage your children to listen for the differences between the correct and incorrect usages.

☐ Practice **Rewriting Sentences** to change the subject and verb forms. For example, have your children practice rewriting sentences from their dictation, changing the noun and verb forms to the opposite of how they were originally. Or you can have them practice *resaying* sentences too. As you're reading a read-aloud to your children, occasionally stop and ask them to repeat a sentence you just read, changing the nouns and verbs to the opposite of the way they're written in the book.

☐ Complete the **Singular/Plural Chart** on **Side A** of the **Lesson 9: Number Student Activity Sheet** by filling in either the plural form of the singular noun given or the singular form of the plural noun given. Remember: Feel free to check the dictionary to confirm the spelling of any nouns you're not sure about.

☐ Get some **Singular/Plural Practice** by analyzing the collective and/or proper nouns listed on **Side B** of the **Lesson 9: Number Student Activity Sheet** and deciding whether each takes a singular or plural verb. Write a creative sentence using each collective and/or proper noun and an appropriate singular or plural verb form. Try to use at least two plural verbs. Remember: Make sure you refer to the *members* of a collective noun rather than to the collective noun as a whole.

Answer Key

Side A: Singular/Plural Chart

1. wishes
2. life
3. cries
4. sisters-in-law
5. cat
6. deer
7. thief
8. woman
9. elves
10. potatoes
11. fry
12. oxen
13. box
14. moose
15. teeth

Side B: Singular/Plural Practice

Answers will vary.

Lesson 10: Person

> **P**ERSON: Person refers to the grammar concept used to distinguish between the speaker of an utterance and those to or about whom he or she is speaking, commonly classified as either first person, second person, or third person.

Teaching Instruction:

In addition to making sure that subjects and verbs agree in number, you also need to make sure that the nouns and pronouns you use in a sentence agree in person. The **person** of a pronoun gives more information about the pronoun.

When two people are communicating, whoever is speaking is called the **first person**, whoever is being spoken to is called the **second person**, and anyone or anything being spoken about is called the **third person**.

First person refers to one's self or to one's own group. If I'm talking about myself, then I am speaking in the first person. Here are some examples of common first person pronouns:

> I, me, my/mine
> we, us, our/ours

Only people who are talking use these pronouns.

Second person refers to the person or group to whom you are speaking. The second person pronouns are:

> you, your, yours

A speaker will use these pronouns only to refer to the person[s] to whom he is speaking.

Third person refers to anyone or anything being spoken about. There are many pronouns for the third person. Which one you use depends on: (1) the number and gender of the thing you're talking about; (2) whether what you're talking about is a person or a thing; and (3) whether it is the subject or the object of your conversation. For example, here are some examples of common third-person pronouns:

> he, him, his
> she, her, hers
> they, them, their/theirs
> it, its

A speaker will use these words only to refer to people/things not part of the conversation.

On the following page, you will find a chart to use for your information and reference. Make sure your children study it and understand the information within it. However, do not make them memorize it or test them based upon it. It is provided only to reinforce the concepts taught in this lesson. It should prove particularly helpful when discussing the many different third-person pronouns and the rules that govern their use.

Notes:

Person/Number	Subject	Possessive	Object
1st/Singular	*I* went to bed.	That is *my* bed.	That hurt *me*.
1st/Plural	*We* went to bed.	Those are *our* beds.	That hurt *us*.
2nd/Singular	*You* went to bed.	That is *your* bed.	That hurt *you*.
2nd/Plural	*You* went to bed.	Those are *your* beds.	That hurt *you*.
3rd/Singular Masculine	*He* went to bed.	That is *his* bed.	That hurt *him*.
3rd/Singular Feminine	*She* went to bed.	That is *her* bed.	That hurt *her*.
3rd/Singular Neuter	*It* went to bed.	That is *its* bed.	That hurt *it*.
3rd/Plural	*They* went to bed.	Those are *their* beds.	That hurt *them*.

In A Nutshell:

Person distinguishes between a speaker, those to whom he is speaking, and those people or things about which he is speaking.

First person = whoever is speaking
Second person = whoever is being spoken to
Third person = anyone or anything being spoken about

Application:

Choose several activities to do over the course of the week to reinforce what you've taught your children about first-, second-, and third-person pronouns:

☐ Review *Rufus Xavier Sarsaparilla* on your *Grammar Rock* DVD.

☐ If you're in a silly mood, have some fun with your children by referring to yourself and them in the **Third Person** for a while. Let's say your name is "George" and your children's names are "Jerry" and "Elaine," just for the sake of this example. A fun conversation with the kids might include such gems as: "Jerry had better pick up his toys. George is getting angry!" "It's time for Elaine to eat. George says 'Hurry up!'" "It has now reached the hour for Jerry and Elaine to go to the library with George. George needs a new book to read." While this exercise is indeed fun in and of itself, do take the opportunity to turn it into a learning experience, by all means. As you laugh with your children as they point out your weird speech, ask them to replace "George," "Jerry," and "Elaine" with appropriate pronouns—and tell you what person they are.

☐ The concept of nouns and pronouns agreeing in number and person is probably new to your children. To help them **Solidify the Concepts** in their minds, pick out a couple of excerpts from books they're reading, either readers or read-alouds, and help them analyze them. Look closely at the text.

What nouns and pronouns are used? Do they agree in number and person? Have them identify the person (first, second, or third) of the pronouns used.

☐ Try your hand at **Fixing Sentences** on **Side A** of the **Lesson 10: Person Student Activity Sheet**. Analyze the sentences listed to determine whether their subjects and verbs and nouns and pronouns agree in number and person. Here's a hint: You're likely to find many problems! Please rewrite the sentences so that: (1) the reader does not have to guess about the pronouns' antecedents; (2) all nouns and pronouns agree in person and number; and (3) all verbs agree with their subjects.

☐ Play **Pick the Pronoun** on **Side B** of the **Lesson 10: Person Student Activity Sheet**. Each of the sentences listed needs some work. The author wasn't sure which pronoun to use in certain spots, so he just took a couple of guesses for each one. Read each sentence and then circle the pronoun that agrees in number and/or person with its antecedent.

Answer Key

Side A: Fixing Sentences

Answers will vary. Possible answers include:

1. Loretta gave her mother jars that her mother couldn't use. Do you think her mother threw them away?

2. Dogs' hairs can make you sneeze. But that doesn't mean you should get rid of dogs. After all, dogs are "man's best friend."

3. The jet engines made such loud noises that the city council wanted to outlaw them. At the next city council meeting, the engines were so noisy that no one could hear themselves think. That was the end of it. The city council voted to outlaw the jet engines.

Side B: Pick the Pronoun

1. They, them, her
2. her, He, them
3. He, it, them
4. They, he, his
5. He, he
6. They, it, their
7. Their, its

Notes:

Lesson 11: Verb Tense

> **V**ERB TENSE: Verb tense refers to a category of verbal inflection that primarily serves to specify the time of the action or state expressed by the verb.

Teaching Instruction:

A verb's **tense** tells you whether an action took place in the past (**past**), is taking place right now (**present**), or will take place in the future (**future**). Verb tense can also tell you whether the action simply happens (**simple**), keeps happening over a period of time (**continuing**), or has concluded prior to the time frame of which we are now speaking (**perfect**). With all of these variables, we can speak of actions taking place in any one of a dozen or more tenses!

Here is a chart that shows several of the tenses for the verb *walk*. As always, don't make your children memorize this chart. Its purpose is merely to help them understand these concepts. By the way, when you put together a list like this that shows the various tenses of a verb, the list is called a **conjugation**. To conjugate a verb means to show its different forms, based on tense.

Verb Conjugations			
Verb Tense:		**Example:**	**Concept:**
Past	Perfect	he *had walked*	before sometime in the past
	Simple	he *walked*	sometime in the past
	Continuing	he *was walking*	for a period of time in the past
Present	Perfect	he *has walked*	before now
	Simple	he *walks*	now
	Continuing	he *is walking*	for some period of time right now
Future	Perfect	he *will have walked*	after now, but before sometime in the near future
	Simple	he *will walk*	sometime in the future
	Continuing	he *will be walking*	for a period of time in the future

As you can see in the chart, many tenses require more than just some form of the root verb; they require helping or auxiliary verbs, such as had, has, was, will have, or will be. You'll learn more about these types of verbs in a future lesson.

Notes:

In A Nutshell:

Verb tense tells you whether an action took place in the past (**past**), is taking place right now (**present**), or will take place in the future (**future**). Verb tense also tells you whether the action simply happens (**simple**), keeps happening over a period of time (**continuing**), or has concluded prior to the time frame of which we are now speaking (**perfect**).

Just For Fun!

For a break, have some fun with your children (and spur their imagination) by discussing onomatopoeia and palindromes.

Onomatopoeia means a word that imitates the sound it represents. Here are a few examples:

buzz
purr
boom
crash
splash

Challenge your children to come up with some more examples of their own.

A **palindrome** is a word, or group of words, that spells the same thing frontward and backward. For example:

mom
pop
gag
race car
Hannah
Stanley Yelnats

What other palindromes can your children think of? Encourage them to try to make up short sentences that are palindromes.

Application:

Choose several activities to do over the course of the week to reinforce what you've taught your children about verb tenses:

☐ Review *A Noun is A Person Place Or Thing, Verb: That's What's Happening,* and *The Tale Of Mr. Morton* on your *Grammar Rock* DVD.

☐ **Keep an "Ear" Out** for your children's use of verbs in their speech. Verb tense is a skill that is easy to work on orally. Throughout the week (and far into the future), listen for mistakes in verb tenses. When you hear them, gently correct them and turn the lesson into a learning opportunity.

☐ As you read with your children, play **Retell That Story**. Select a short passage for your children to read. Ask them to identify what verb tenses the author used. Then challenge your children to repeat the passage in a different tense. For example, was the author describing a past event? Retell it as something to occur in the future.

☐ Write a **Letter to an Old Friend**. If you can't think of a friend to write to, you can make up an imaginary friend or write to a parent or relative. In this letter, write one paragraph about what you've been doing (past), one paragraph about what you're doing right now (present), and one paragraph about what you plan to do soon (future). Concentrate on using the appropriate verb tenses throughout the letter.

☐ **Conjugate That Verb!** by filling in the missing verb forms in the chart on **Side A** of the <u>**Lesson 11: Verb Tense**</u> **Student Activity Sheet.** Feel free to refer to the chart in the *Teaching Instruction* section if you need help.

☐ Read the sentences on **Side B** of the <u>**Lesson 11: Verb Tense**</u> **Student Activity Sheet** and use the **Timing Clues** given to fill in the blanks with verbs with the correct tense.

Answer Key

Side A: Conjugate That Verb!

1. he smiled
2. he was smiling
3. he has smiled
4. he smiles
5. he is smiling
6. he will smile
7. he will be smiling

Side B: Timing Clues

Answers will vary. Possible answers include:

1. fixed
2. will have
3. will pull
4. hit
5. likes
6. will do
7. watched, talked
8. carries

Lesson 12: Voice

> **V**OICE: Voice is a grammatical term typically used to indicate the relation of the verbal action to the subject as performer or beneficiary of its action.

Voice is a grammatical term used to describe whether the subject of a sentence is acting (active voice) or being acted upon (passive voice). **Active-voice** sentences always tell you who did the action. The subject comes first, and the subject does the action. For example:

> The sloth slept in the tree.
> The monkey threw a large coconut.
> The sloth fell to the ground with a thud.

In **passive-voice** sentences, the subject of the sentence is acted upon, but does not act. The subject of the sentence is the object of the verb. For example:

> The sloth was felled by a tropical fruit.
> The fruit was propelled by the monkey's fist.
> The tree was vacated suddenly by the rudely-awakened sloth.

If a sentence doesn't tell you *who* is doing the action, it must be a passive sentence:

> The bananas were stolen.

Who stole them? To make this sentence active, we must tell who stole the bananas:

> The bananas were stolen by the monkey.

"Wait a second! That still sounds passive." If that's what you were just thinking, you'd be right. There's one more thing we forgot. To make a passive sentence active, you must not only tell *who* does the action, but you must make sure that you have the *subject* do the action! Let's try this one more time:

> The monkey stole the bananas.

So what do you think? Which sentence is better? The passive one we started with *(The bananas were stolen.)* or the active sentence we finished with *(The monkey stole the bananas.)*? The active-voice sentence gives more information and has a life to it that the passive-voice sentence lacks.

To write well, use a lot of active-voice sentences. It's not necessary to avoid all passive-voice sentences, but keep in mind that when subjects don't do anything it slows things down and weakens the meaning.

So how do you make sure that you're writing in the active voice? It takes time and a concerted effort to edit your work carefully. When you're done with a draft of something you're writing, look over it carefully. Are your subjects clear and are they doing the acting?

Also pay close attention to your verbs. Your sentences are most likely in the passive voice if they include some form of the verb *to be*. Remember: Try to replace as many *to be's* as you can with other, more active verbs.

Verbals are also good indicators of passive-voice sentences. Verbals are words derived from verbs that act as another part of speech. Verbals include gerunds, participles, and infinitives. We will cover verbals in more detail in later lessons. For now, it is sufficient to have just a very basic understanding of verbals, so that you can spot them in order to ferret out any passive-voice sentences in your writing.

Gerunds are verb forms that end in –*ing* and act as nouns. **Participles** are verb forms that usually end in -*ing* or -*ed* and act as adjectives. **Infinitives** are verb forms that usually begin with the word *to* and act as nouns, adjectives, or adverbs. For example, the verb *run* can be transformed into a gerund (*Running* is my favorite sport.), a participle (The boys *running* around the track were very tired.), and an infinitive (If it were easy *to run* a marathon, I'd run one tomorrow!).

Here are a few last rules to keep in mind:

1. You can be quite sure that if you use many participles, you are writing in the passive voice. Avoid participial phrases if at all possible.

2. If you find a gerund in a sentence, you can be quite sure that you are writing in the passive voice. Get rid of gerunds whenever possible.

3. If at all possible, only use the verb *to be* with regular nouns and regular adjectives.

In A Nutshell:

Voice refers to whether the subject of a sentence is acting (active voice) or being acted upon (passive voice).

Active-voice sentences always tell you who did the action. The subject comes first, and the subject does the action.

In **passive-voice** sentences, the subject of the sentence is acted upon, but does not act.

Application:

Choose several activities to do over the course of the week to reinforce what you've taught your children about the active and passive voice:

☐ Review ***Verb: That's What's Happening*** or any of the other songs we've covered already on your ***Grammar Rock*** DVD.

☐ Even if you can't sing, you can still be a **Voice Coach**! Grab a few of your children's recent writing samples. Ask them to do another edit of them, trying to spot passive sentences. How did they do? Are there many? Don't worry if there are. Writing in the active voice is a skill that takes practice. Challenge them to turn all of their passive-voice sentences into active-voice sentences that sing!

☐ Play **Newspaper Editor** with your children. Let them be the editor and you pretend to be the rookie reporter. Find a few short newspaper articles from a local paper or online and submit them to your editor for review. In the role of editor, your children should carefully analyze the articles you've submitted for active- and passive-voice sentences. Ask them to point out passive-voice sentences they find. They should also suggest how any passive-voice sentences they find can be changed to make them active.

☐ Read the sentences in the chart on **Side A** of the **Lesson 12: Voice Student Activity Sheet**. Are they **Active or Passive?** Do you remember how to tell? If you need to, please feel free to refer back to the ***Teaching Instructions*** for help. Place an "X" in the proper column after each sentence to denote whether it's active or passive.

☐ We're having some trouble writing active-voice sentences. Take a look at the sentences on **Side B** of the **Lesson 12: Voice** **Student Activity Sheet.** They're pathetic. They need some **Action!** Please help us fix them. Rewrite them in *active voice* and, if you need to, please feel free to provide a subject for the sentence.

Answer Key

Side A: Active or Passive?

1. Active
2. Passive
3. Active
4. Passive
5. Passive
6. Active
7. Passive
8. Active
9. Passive
10. Active

Side B: Action!

Answers will vary. Possible answers include:

1. Mom walked the dogs.
2. Loretta spotted the angel.
3. Everyone appreciated the music.
4. Jim launched twelve rockets.
5. Stephanie scolded Doug.
6. The nail flattened the tire.
7. Sally had squashed three armadillos.
8. The mayor dedicated the library.

Lesson 13: Synonyms & Antonyms

> **S**YNONYM: A synonym is a word having the same or nearly the same meaning as another in a language.
>
> **A**NTONYM: An antonym is a word having the opposite or nearly the opposite meaning as another in a language.

Teaching Instruction:

In this lesson, we're going to take a quick look at the related concepts of synonyms and antonyms. Although simple on their face, these concepts can be a critical component in the development of your children's writing abilities.

Synonyms are words that have the same (or nearly the same) meaning. For example:

> big—large
> little—small
> laugh—chuckle

Antonyms are words that have the opposite (or nearly the opposite) meaning. For example:

> up—down
> cold—hot
> out—in

While it probably will be easy for your children to understand these new terms, applying them to their writing will likely prove to be more difficult. Please help your children enliven their writing assignments by replacing tired, common words with synonyms that sing! Or help them rephrase things in an opposite manner by using creative antonyms. Simply thinking about synonyms and antonyms as they write will help your children to create pieces that are more fun and interesting to read.

In A Nutshell:

Synonyms are words that have the same (or nearly the same) meaning.

Antonyms are words that have the opposite (or nearly the opposite) meaning.

Application:

Choose several activities to do over the course of the week to reinforce what you've taught your children about synonyms and antonyms:

☐ Review any of the songs we've covered already on your ***Grammar Rock*** DVD.

☐ Pick out one or two recent writing assignments for your children to review. Challenge them to think of synonyms and antonyms for some of the more common words in their sentences. Can they make their writing better by replacing some of these words with synonyms or rewriting some of the sentences in a way that features an antonym instead? Explain to them that this critical process is called **"Editing"** and that all great writers do it to improve their writing.

☐ One day this week, inform your children (first thing in the morning!) that it is **Opposite Day**. On opposite day, your children must say the opposite of what they really intend to say. Do they feel great? If so, they should tell you how awful they feel. Do they want grilled cheese for lunch? If not, they should definitely tell you "Yes!" What about the weather? Is it sunny outside? Your children should talk about the bad weather then. This fun game will give your children plenty of practice with antonyms …and lead to some fairly hilarious conversations throughout the day. Some advice: Opposite Day may best be practiced indoors. Opposite Day conversations in the grocery store may lead to strange stares from your friends and neighbors!

☐ In the **Brainstorm** chart on **Side A** of the <u>**Lesson 13: Synonyms &**</u> <u>**Antonyms**</u> **Student Activity Sheet**, we've listed some common words. For each word, your children should list at least two synonyms and two antonyms in the appropriate columns. If they can think of more than two, they should list as many as they can. Encourage them to be as creative as they can. For example, "large" is a synonym for "big," but it's not very creative. "Humongous" would be a much more descriptive synonym.

☐ Try **Sprucing Up** each of the rather plain sentences on **Side B** of the <u>**Lesson 13: Synonyms & Antonyms**</u> **Student Activity Sheet**. Each sentence needs to be rewritten, replacing any underlined words with either synonyms or antonyms that are more creative. Try to use synonyms about half the time and antonyms about half the time. Encourage your children to be as creative as they can. Changing the meaning of the sentence is fine as long as they give the reader something interesting to read!

Answer Key

Side A: Brainstorm

Answers will vary. Possible answers include:

	Synonyms:	Antonyms:
1. big		small, tiny
2. beautiful	attractive, gorgeous	homely, hideous
3. quickly	expeditious, speedily	slowly, sluggishly
4. hungry	famished, starved	stuffed, satisfied
5. tired	weary, exhausted	energized, vigorous
6. poor	destitute, broke	wealthy, rich
7. skinny	slender, scrawny	rotund, chubby
8. happy	delighted, joyful	
9. completely	thoroughly, totally	barely, partially
10. dark	black, gloomy	bright, sunny

Side B: Sprucing Up

Answers will vary. Possible answers include:

1. Sue Ellen Miske *was depressed* because her friend moved to Indiana.
2. The Christmas shoppers waited in line *forever* for the new *board* game.
3. Buford Badger built a *substantial* bridge across the bubbling *stream*.
4. Jerry played a *joke* on his mailman.
5. A hedgehog *noisily* hid in the bushes across the *street*.
6. The *hurricane* moved across the *peninsula*.
7. Helen *loved* to play her harmonica *after dinner*.

Lesson 14: Predicate Nouns & Adjectives

> **P**REDICATE NOUN: Predicate nouns are nouns used in the predicate to refer to or otherwise describe or identify the subject.
>
> **P**REDICATE ADJECTIVE: Predicate adjectives are adjectives used in the predicate after a linking verb to describe the subject or direct object.

Teaching Instruction:

In an earlier lesson, we discussed nouns in the context of the subject of a sentence. In this lesson, we'll learn that nouns can also appear in the predicate. A **predicate noun** is a noun that comes after a linking verb (you'll learn more about linking verbs in a later lesson) and defines or describes the subject of a sentence. For example:

> Frogs are *amphibians*.
> Turkeys are *birds*.

In these sentences, *are* is the linking verb and *amphibians* and *birds* are the predicate nouns.

Linking verbs can also be followed by adjectives. A **predicate adjective** is an adjective that comes after a linking verb and modifies or describes the subject of a sentence. For example:

> Rutabagas are *bitter*.
> The water seems *clear*.

In these sentences, *are* and *seems* are the linking verbs and *bitter* and *clear* are the predicate adjectives. Common linking verbs include: is, are, was, am, seems, feel, smell, grow, stay, etc.

In A Nutshell:

Predicate nouns are nouns that come after a linking verb and define or describe the subject of a sentence.

Predicate adjectives are adjectives that come after a linking verb and modify or describe the subject of a sentence.

Just For Fun!

An **idiom** is a group of words that paints a mental picture that means something totally different from what the words themselves imply. Idioms are also known as figures of speech. Some idioms can sound quite silly if you don't recognize them for what they are. For example:

> Phil was *pulling my leg*.

Personification means giving an inanimate object human qualities. For example:

> The wind moaned and breathed, speaking to all that winter is here.

Notes:

Application:

Choose several activities to do over the course of the week to reinforce what you've taught your children about predicate nouns and predicate adjectives:

☐ Review **The Tale Of Mr. Morton** or any of the other songs we've covered already on your **Grammar Rock** DVD.

☐ Help your children do some more **Editing** of their recent writing assignments. Identifying predicate nouns and predicate adjectives is a good way to improve your children's writing. Predicate nouns and predicate adjectives require linking verbs, which are passive—they don't do anything except link subjects with nouns and adjectives. So pick out a couple of your children's recent writing samples and ask them to look for predicate nouns and predicate adjectives. Let's say they find a predicate adjective: The horse is beautiful. Ask them to improve this sentence. Move the predicate adjective to the subject—the beautiful horse—and then have the subject do something: The beautiful horse prances. This kind of editing will turn boring, bland sentences into something their readers will enjoy.

☐ Have your children **Write 10 Sentences** that feature either a predicate noun or a predicate adjective. When they're finished, have them rewrite the sentences, using the predicate noun or predicate adjective in a new way without the linking verb.

☐ Practice **Combining Sentences**. Read each pair of sentences on **Side A** of the **Lesson 14: Predicate Nouns & Adjectives** Student Activity Sheet. Write PN over any predicate nouns and PA over any predicate adjectives you identify. Then rewrite the sentences, combining each pair into one better, more active sentence.

☐ **Finish the Sentences** on **Side B** of the **Lesson 14: Predicate Nouns & Adjectives Student Activity Sheet** with a creative predicate noun or predicate adjective. Then write a new sentence using the predicate noun or predicate adjective in a new way without the linking verb.

Answer Key

Side A: Combining Sentences

1. The _yellow_ dog chased a cat up the tree. *(PA)*
2. Should we swim in the _murky_ stream? *(PA)*
3. The _tired_ boys ran all the way home from school. *(PA)*
4. Jennifer, the _leader_, organizes the meetings. *(PN)*
5. The _young_ girls played on the swing set in their yard. *(PA)*
6. The _huge_ elephant balanced on a beach ball. *(PA)*
7. His _fast_ car raced through the stoplight. *(PA)*

Side B: Finish the Sentences

Answers will vary. Possible answers include:

1. The _friendly_ three bears invited the little girl into their home.
2. The _rushed_ waiter spilled water all over the table.
3. His _neglected_ farm needed a significant amount of work.
4. The *beautiful* antelope ran across the road.
5. _Sad_ Loretta sat on her couch alone
6. The _tired_ mailman took a break in the shade.
7. Her _lost_ sheep wandered off to find water.
8. Jeffrey, who is _the boss_, gave a speech to motivate the company.

Lesson 15: Prepositions

> **P**REPOSITION: Prepositions are words that are used before nouns or pronouns to form phrases functioning as modifiers of verbs, nouns, or adjectives, usually expressing a spatial, temporal, or other relationship.

Teaching Instruction:

A **preposition** tells you *where*, *when*, or *how* something takes place. Most prepositions indicate direction or position. Some common prepositions are: on, at, in, around, through, away, from, under, over, up, down, etc. Here are some examples of prepositions in sentences:

> Christian was a waiter *at* the hotel.
> Sandy found a quarter *in* the sand.
> Wanda went *to* her friend's house.

Four prepositions—*of*, *by*, *for*, and *with*—don't indicate direction or position. However, they speak of *logical relations* between things. For example:

> Life is like a box *of* chocolates.
> I will stand *by* you.
> Friends are *for* life.
> Randy went to Mexico *with* Linda.

Prepositions normally require an object—a noun—called **the object of the preposition**. The object of the preposition tells you the *cause* of the action or *where* it takes place (or *by whom* or *what* it happens). For example:

> The cow jumped over the *moon*.
> The spoon dropped to the *floor*.

In these sentences, *moon* and *floor* are the objects of the prepositions *over* and *to*.

A preposition and its object, together (plus any adjectives and adverbs that may help to describe the object), are called a **prepositional phrase**. In the last example, the complete prepositional phrases are *over the moon* and *to the floor*. The phrases include the prepositions *over* and *to*, the objects *moon* and *floor*, and the adjective (article) *the*.

Prepositional phrases almost always serve as adjectives or adverbs. In the last example, *over the moon* serves as an adverb modifying the verb *jumped* and *to the floor* serves as an adverb modifying the verb *dropped*.

Some prepositions consist of more than one word. Many of these multi-word prepositions include the word *of*. Examples include: because of, in front of, and to the side of.

Prepositions can also serve as adverbs when there is no object of the preposition. Grammarians speak of these verb-modifying prepositions as either adverbs or parts of phrasal verbs. Here are a couple of examples of these types of prepositions:

> Karleen put the coffee cup *down*.
> Hannah looked *up*.

Notes:

To help you identify prepositions, here is a fairly comprehensive list of the most common ones. As always, this list is for reference only:

Common Prepositions							
aboard	about	above	according to	across	across from	after	against
along	alongside	alongside of	along with	amid	among	apart from	around
aside from	at	away from	because of	before	behind	below	beneath
beside	besides	between	beyond	by	by means of		concerning
considering		despite	down	down from	during	except	except for
excepting	for	for	from among	from between	from under	in	in addition to
in back of	in behalf of		in front of	in place of	in regard to	inside	inside of
in spite of	instead of	into	like	near	near to	of	off
on	on account of	on behalf of	onto	on top of	opposite	out	out of
outside	outside of	over	over to	owing to	past	prior to	regarding
round	round about	save	since	subsequent to		through	throughout
till	to	together	toward	toward	underneath		until
until	unto	up	up to	upon	with	within	without

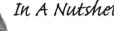

In A Nutshell:

Prepositions tells you *where*, *when*, or *how* something takes place. Most prepositions indicate direction or position.

The **object of the preposition**—a noun—tells you the *cause* of the action or *where* it takes place (or *by whom* or *what* it happens).

A preposition and its object, together (plus any adjectives and adverbs that may help to describe the object), are called a **prepositional phrase**.

Application:

Choose several activities to do over the course of the week to reinforce what you've taught your children about prepositions:

☐ Watch *Busy Prepositions* on your *Grammar Rock* **DVD**. Feel free to watch this particular lesson several times throughout the week, as repetition will enhance your children's ability to remember the concept later.

☐ Encourage your children to so some more **Editing** of their recent work. Have they been using prepositions and prepositional phrases without realizing it? Can they identify any prepositions, objects of prepositions, or prepositional phrases in their writing? If so, have them mark these items. If not, can they spice up their writing by adding additional details via prepositions and prepositional phrases? Remember: Prepositional phrases generally serve as adjectives or adverbs, so adding them will help make your children's writing sparkle!

☐ Ask your children to play **Newspaper Editor** again. Find a few short newspaper articles from a local paper or online and submit them to your children for review. In the role of editor, your children should carefully analyze the articles you've submitted for prepositions, objects of prepositions, and prepositional phrases. Ask them to circle the prepositions, put a star above the objects of prepositions, and underline the complete prepositional phrases they find. If you want, you can also challenge them to identify how the prepositional phrases are used in the sentences. Are they serving as adjectives or adverbs? What words do they modify?

☐ OK, detectives! Put on your tweed coats and grab your magnifying glasses. It's time to play **Prepositional Sleuth** on **Side A** of the <u>**Lesson 15: Prepositions** Student Activity Sheet</u>. Analyze the sentences to find some prepositions and prepositional phrases. Circle the prepositions and underline the complete prepositional phrases.

☐ It's time for your children to be creative and apply what they've learned about prepositions and prepositional phrases by writing some **Preposentences**. The chart on **Side B** of the <u>**Lesson 15: Prepositions** Student Activity Sheet</u> contains prepositions and nouns that can be objects of prepositions.Challenge your children to mix and match these prepositions and objects to form prepositional phrases. Then have them write five sentences featuring their combinations. When they're done, have them circle the prepositions and underline the complete prepositional phrases.

Notes:

Side A: Prepositional Sleuth

1. Snow White lived (in) the seven dwarves' house.
2. Buddy went (to) the camping store.
3. Frank slid (into) his warm sleeping bag.
4. The salamander ate the pancake (in) less than ten seconds.
5. Jake went (to) work by taxi.
6. Sandy was shy (because of) her accent.
7. Barry landed the helicopter (on top of) the burning building.

Side B: Preposentences

Answers will vary.

Lesson 16: Indirect Objects

> **I**NDIRECT OBJECT: Indirect objects are words or groups of words representing the person or thing with reference to which the action of a verb is performed, usually coming between the verb and the direct object.

Teaching Instruction:

An **indirect object** receives the action of a verb indirectly. In other words, it receives the action *after* the direct object receives it and as a *result* of the direct object having received the action. (If you need to, feel free to review Lesson 8 for more information about direct objects.) Here are a few examples that will help you understand the concept of indirect objects:

Duane threw *Amber* the chipmunk.

What did Duane throw? Amber? Of course not! He threw the chipmunk *to* Amber. *Amber*—the indirect object here—receives the chipmunk as a result of the chipmunk receiving the direct action of being thrown.

With much trepidation, Gary handed *Zachary* the keys.

In this sentence, the keys are the direct object; they are what receive the direct action of being handed. *Zachary* is the indirect object, because he receives the keys as a result of the keys having received the direct action of being handed.

NOTE: Although a prepositional phrase may tell you the same information that an indirect object does (Gary handed the keys *to Zachary.*), a prepositional phrase is never an indirect object. It always remains a prepositional phrase.

In A Nutshell:

Indirect objects receive the action from a verb indirectly—*after* the direct object receives it and as a *result* of the direct object having received the action.

Application:

Choose several activities to do over the course of the week to reinforce what you've taught your children about indirect objects:

☐ Review any or all of the songs on your **Grammar Rock** DVD that we've covered thus far.

☐ Challenge your children to become **Newspaper Sleuths**. Browse through a local newspaper to find a few child-friendly articles. Then ask your children to read the articles and circle as many indirect objects as they can find. If that's too easy for them, ask them to find subjects, verbs, adjectives, adverbs, direct objects, and/or prepositions too.

☐ Play an exciting game of **The Mischievous Mole.** Make up some sentences about what the mischievous mole might do, and then have your children finish the sentences with creative indirect objects and direct objects. For example, if you say, "The mischievous mole gave," then your children might say, "the pig a magazine." Other verbs you can try: handed, offered, threw,

Notes:

sent, fetched, tossed, etc. Feel free to make up your own creative verbs. For a variation, challenge your children to add colorful adjectives and adverbs as well.

☐ Ask your children to **Pick and Choose** subjects, verbs, indirect objects, and direct objects from the chart on **Side A** of the **Lesson 16: Indirect Objects Student Activity Sheet**, and then use them to create five crazy sentences. Note: They can mix and match the subjects, verbs, indirect objects, and direct objects however they like. They do not have to put together sentences using all the words in any particular row. They do, however, need to make sure that they use each word no more than once. Have fun!

☐ Complete the **Label That Sentence** exercise on **Side B** of the **Lesson 16: Indirect Objects Student Activity Sheet**. Each of the sentences listed contains a subject, a verb, an indirect object, and a direct object. Label each subject with "S," each verb with "V," each indirect object with "IO," and each direct object with "DO." For a challenge, label any adjectives with "ADJ" and any adverbs with "ADV."

Answer Key

Side A: Pick and Choose

Answers will vary.

Side B: Label That Sentence

    adj   s   v   adj io adj adj do
1. The armadillo handed the rabbit the car keys.

    s   v   io adj adj   DO
2. Pa fetched Ma a copper kettle.

    s   v   io   adj adj   do
3. Alice offered Melinda the cold leftovers.

    s   v adj   io   adj adj   do
4. Deb sent the Densmers a thank-you gift.

    adj   s   v   io   adj adj   do
5. The mailman tossed Old Man Jenkins his afternoon paper.

    s   v adj adj   io adj adj   do
6. Jerry threw his friend Elaine the golden scepter.

    adj   s   v   adj   io   adj do
7. Twelve raccoons passed the elephants a football.

    s   v   io adj   adj adj do
8. Jean built John a fabulous log cabin.

Lesson 17: Appositives

> **A**PPOSITIVE: Appositives are words or phrases placed in apposition, or directly following, the nouns or pronouns they modify.

Teaching Instruction:

An **appositive** is a noun or noun phrase (**appositive phrase**) that renames or describes the nouns or pronouns that come immediately before it. Appositives are usually surrounded—or set off by—commas. For example:

> The man behind the counter, *George*, is the butcher.
> My guitar, *an Ibanez*, has an electric blue flame on it.
> Mark, *first baseman for the Rangers*, had a strong season.
> Carmen, *a mother of three*, barely had time to make dinner.

In the sentences above, the italicized words and phrases are appositives or appositive phrases. Do you see how they rename or describe the nouns that come before them?

You should use an appositive or an appositive phrase when you want to say something important about the subject, but you want the sentence itself to focus on something even more important. For example, let's say you want to say that *David defeated the Philistine warrior with a single stone*. That's your main message. But you realize that, in order for them to really understand what you are saying, you also need to tell them that he was just a young boy. How can you do that? Use an appositive like this:

> David, *a young boy*, defeated the Philistine warrior with a single stone.

In A Nutshell:

Appositives are nouns or noun phrases (**appositive phrases**) that rename or describe the nouns or pronouns that come immediately before them. Appositives are surrounded—or set off by—commas.

Application:

Choose several activities to do over the course of the week to reinforce what you've taught your children about appositives:

☐ Review any or all of the songs on your ***Grammar Rock*** DVD that we've covered thus far.

☐ Play **Add an Appositive** this week. Make up 10-15 crazy sentences. You can write them down or just say them to your children. Then ask your children to add appositives to your crazy sentences. They can either write them down or say them. It's up to you. For example, you might say, "Doris and Boris love to eat pickle soup." Your children might then respond, "Doris and Boris, *our foreign exchange students from Picklestan*, love to eat pickle soup."

☐ Play a variation of the **Word Association** game. You say a noun (a subject) and have your children respond—as quickly as possible—with the first appositive they think of. Then let them finish the sentence in any way they choose Explain to them that they need to say an appositive—a noun or noun phrase that describes or renames the subject—rather than an adjective. For example: you say "Elmer"; they say "*the little pig . . . wallowed in the mud.*" Have fun!

☐ We have **A Positively Fun Activity** on **Side A** of the **Lesson 17: Appositives Student Activity Sheet**. The sentences listed there are incomplete. Each one needs some critical information filled in. Have your children read the sentences as they are and then fill in each blank with an appositive or an appositive phrase. Encourage them to be silly if they want! The more funny and creative their sentences are, the more their readers will enjoy them.

☐ Challenge your children to **Combine the Sentences** on **Side B** of the **Lesson 17: Appositives** Student Activity Sheet. Each pair of sentences listed can be combined into one sentence featuring an appositive or appositive phrase. Ask your children to read the sentences and then rewrite them as one sentence, turning the less important sentence into an appositive or an appositive phrase.

Answer Key

Side A: A Positively Fun Activity

Answers will vary.

Side B: Combine the Sentences

1. The ducks, Huey, Dewey, and Louie, were in big trouble after breaking the precious vase.
2. Hannah, usually a well-behaved baby, was throwing a temper tantrum because no one was paying attention to her.
3. Sammy, the manager, spied on the workers as they ate lunch.

Lesson 18: Phrases

> PHRASE: A phrase is a sequence of two or more words that does not contain a finite verb and its subject or that does not consist of clause elements such as subject, verb, object, or complement, as a preposition and a noun or pronoun, an adjective and noun, or an adverb and verb.

Teaching Instruction:

A **phrase** is a group of related words that is missing a subject (noun), a predicate (verb), or both. A phrase always has two or more words but is never a complete sentence. If a group of words contains both a subject and a predicate, then it's a clause or a sentence rather than a phrase. You've already seen some examples of phrases: prepositional phrases, appositive phrases, etc.

The words in a phrase express meaning within a clause or sentence. Phrases commonly fulfill the function of a single part of speech—a noun, a verb, an adjective, an adverb, etc. Here are some examples of phrases:

> *under the circus tent*
> *climbing the ladder*
> *swinging from the trapeze*

Under the circus tent is a prepositional phrase that could be used in a sentence as an adjective to describe where something is or as an adverb to describe where something is occurring.

Climbing the ladder is a participial phrase in which *the ladder* is the object of the participle *climbing*, and the participle *climbing* is an adjective. There is no subject or predicate.

Swinging from the trapeze is a gerund phrase that could be used as the subject of a sentence.

There are many types of phrases. Don't worry about naming the various types of phrases and analyzing the role they play in sentences yet. It will be sufficient for now simply to work on identifying phrases as groups of words that are missing a subject (noun), a predicate (verb), or both.

In A Nutshell:

Phrases are group of related words that are missing a subject (noun), a predicate (verb), or both.

A phrase always has two or more words but is never a complete sentence. Phrases commonly fulfill the function of a single part of speech—a noun, a verb, an adjective, an adverb, etc.

Application:

Choose several activities to do over the course of the week to reinforce what you've taught your children about phrases:

- ☐ Review any or all of the songs on your ***Grammar Rock DVD*** that we've covered thus far.

- ☐ Encourage your children to so some more **Editing** of their recent work. Can they identify phrases in their writing? If so, have them underline them.

Discuss the phrases they find. What kind are they? How are they functioning in the sentences they're in? Can your children rewrite any sentences with participial or gerund phrases to make them more active?

☐ Review the **Student Activity Sheets** your children completed for the lessons on prepositions and appositives. Walk through the sheets with your children, using them to reinforce what they've just learned about phrases in general. If they want to, let them re-do any of the activities from those lessons.

☐ Engage in some **Phraseology** on **Side A** of the **Lesson 18: Phrases Student Activity Sheet**. Sometimes we have some great ideas that just seem never to get finished. For example, we've come up with some really great phrases recently. We wanted to turn them into fabulous sentences, but we never got around to it. Can your children help us? Can they turn each of the phrases into a super, spectacular sentence?

☐ Challenge your children to **Underline the Phrases** in the sentences on **Side B** of the **Lesson 18: Phrases** Student Activity Sheet. Each of the sentences contains one or more phrases of various types. Ask them to read the sentences and underline all of the phrases they find. If they're up for a challenge, encourage them to try to identify the kinds of phrases and how they're functioning in the sentences.

Answer Key

Side A: Phraseology

Answers will vary.

Side B: Underline the Phrases

1. beyond the hill *(prepositional phrase/adjective modifying woods)*;
   at night *(prepositional phrase/adverb modifying frightening)*

2. Chasing the cat *(gerund phrase/the subject of the sentence)*

3. over the barn *(prepositional phrase/adverb modifying flew)*

4. Running from the law *(gerund phrase/subject of the sentence)*

5. Blinded by the light *(participle phrase/adjective modifying deer)*;
   in its tracks *(prepositional phrase/adverb modifying halted)*

6. Sliding down the waterslide *(gerund phrase/the subject of the sentence)*

7. swimming in the lake *(participle phrase/describing swans)*

8. coming down in buckets *(participle phrase/describing rain)*;
   off the road *(prepositional phrase/adverb modifying washed)*

9. Flattered by his offer *(participle phrase/describing Josie)*;
   around his neck *(prepositional phrase/adverb modifying threw)*

Lesson 19: Clauses

> **C**LAUSE: A clause is a group of words containing a subject and predicate and forming either part of a sentence or a whole simple sentence.

Teaching Instruction:

A **clause** is a group of related words that includes a subject and a predicate. All complete sentences include at least one clause. Many sentences include two or more clauses. Here are some examples:

> Jonathan slept.
> Pete ate ice cream all night, and he felt sick the next day.

The first sentence is an example of a clause that is also a simple sentence. It contains the bare minimum requirements: a subject (*Jonathan*) and a predicate (*slept*). The second sentence contains two clauses. Can you identify the two subjects? (*Pete* and *he*) The two predicates? (*ate ice cream all night* and *felt sick the next day*)

Some clauses have one subject but two or more predicates. For example:

> Stan *walked* and *jumped*.
> The actress *stumbled at the top of the stairs, almost recovered*, but *fell anyway*.

Some clauses have two or more subjects to whom or to which the same predicates apply. For example:

> The *bobcats* and *coyotes* howled and screeched.
> *Sarah, Jenny,* and *Lisa* crashed into each other and stumbled down the driveway.

Each of the examples above contains just one clause with multiple subjects and/ or predicates. If, however, different predicates apply to different subjects, then you have separate clauses. For example, each of these sentences has two clauses:

> *The bobcat howled* while *the coyote screeched*.
> *Sarah crashed into Jenny*, but *Lisa fell down the stairs*.

As soon as your children are comfortable with the basic concepts set forth above, feel free to move ahead and explain that there are two types of clauses. **Independent clauses** can stand on their own as a sentence because they contain a complete thought. For example:

> Skeeter goes to school.
> Wayne and Sue were too busy to play.

Dependent clauses (also called **subordinate clauses**), on the other hand, do not contain a complete thought and, therefore, cannot stand on their own as a sentence. They are subordinate to—depend on—separate, independent clauses to "hold them up." For example:

> *Because eagles are an endangered species,* the poacher was arrested.
> *Although everyone else wanted to eat Italian food*, Pam held out for green beans.

Notes:

The dependent clauses in the sentences above do not contain complete thoughts. To see so for yourself, try reading them aloud by themselves. You should be able to "hear" how they are incomplete.

What words make the dependent clauses dependent? (*Although* and *Because*) These words are called subordinating conjunctions. Subordinate (or dependent) clauses begin with subordinating conjunctions and do not convey complete thoughts because of the subordinating conjunctions. (See the ***Just for Fun!*** section below for more information about subordinating conjunctions.)

Although it is not necessary to delve this deeply into clauses at this point, feel free to point out to your children that there are three types of dependent (or subordinate) clauses, named after the function they perform: **noun clauses**, **adjective clauses**, and **adverb clauses**. Here is an example of each:

> The boys knew *that the police were after them*.
> [noun clause—direct object]

> *If the boys tell the truth*, things will go much easier for them.
> [adverb clause—modifies *will go*]

> The boys' crime, *which was no longer a secret*, was about to catch up with them.
> [adjective clause—modifies *crime*]

In A Nutshell:

Clauses are groups of related words that include a subject and a predicate.

Independent clauses can stand on their own as a sentence because they contain a complete thought.

Dependent clauses (also called **subordinate clauses**) do not contain a complete thought and cannot stand on their own as a sentence.

Just for Fun!

A **subordinating conjunction** connects two clauses such that one of the clauses depends on the other to make sense. Subordinating conjunctions always come at the beginning of a subordinate (or dependent) clause. For example:

> Joe ran when he saw the bear.

When is the subordinating conjunction. We have to know that *Joe ran* before the clause *when he saw the bear* makes much sense.

Here is a list of some of the most common subordinating conjunctions: after, because, so that, when, although, before, that, where, as, if, though, whereas, as if, in order that, till, while, as long as, provided that, unless, as though, since, and until.

Application:

Choose several activities to do over the course of the week to reinforce what you've taught your children about clauses:

☐ Watch ***Conjunction Junction*** on your ***Grammar Rock*** DVD. Keep an eye out for subordinating conjunctions in particular.

☐ Play **Finish My Sentence**. You say a dependent (or subordinate) clause, and your children finish with an independent clause. Be as silly as you want to be! For example, you might say, "When the bear saw the rollerskates…." and your children might follow with "he jumped for joy and strapped them to his big, furry feet." As you play, reinforce your children's understanding of the differences between independent and dependent clauses.

☐ Challenge your children to be **Clause Spotters**. Give them a newspaper or magazine and ask them to identify 10 independent clauses and 10 dependent clauses.

☐ Help us **Clause-It** on **Side A** of the **Lesson 19: Clauses Student Activity Sheet**. We recently had another batch of great ideas that never got finished. We came up with some wonderful dependent (or subordinate) clauses. However, as you know, dependent (or subordinate) clauses rely on other independent clauses to make sense. Can your children help us turn each of our dependent (or subordinate) clauses into a great sentence?

☐ **Is It A Clause?** Tell us on **Side B** of the **Lesson 19: Clauses Student Activity Sheet**. Ask your children to analyze the groups of words in the chart to determine whether they are independent clauses, dependent clauses, or not clauses at all. Then have them put an "X" in the appropriate column following each group of words.

Answer Key

Side A: Clause-It

Answers will vary.

Side B: Is It A Clause?

1. Not a Clause
2. Independent
3. Dependent
4. Independent
5. Dependent
6. Not a Clause
7. Independent
8. Dependent
9. Not a Clause
10. Not a Clause
11. Independent
12. Dependent
13. Independent
14. Not a Clause
15. Dependent

Notes:

Lesson 20: Types of Sentences

> SENTENCE: A sentence is a grammatical unit of one or more words expressing a complete thought or idea, such as an assertion, a question, a command, a wish, an exclamation, or the performance of an action. Sentences begin with a capital letter and end with proper punctuation.

Teaching Instruction:

Sentences come in many forms: simple, complex, compound, compound-complex, as well as declarative, exclamatory, and interrogative. In this lesson, we will briefly survey the various types of sentences. Remember: Mastery is not essential at this point. Just be sure your children have a basic understanding of these concepts.

One way to classify sentences is based upon how many independent and dependent clauses are present in the sentence. A **simple sentence** contains a single independent clause, though it may have a compound subject and/or a compound predicate. A simple sentence can have one or more phrases, but it cannot have any dependent clauses. Here are some examples of simple sentences:

> The porcupine danced.
> The porcupine and the skunk danced.
> The skunk danced and sang with the porcupine.

A **complex sentence** contains an independent clause and a dependent clause. For example:

> After I go to the gym, I like to go grocery shopping.
> When Gary saw April 1 on his calendar, he broke into a cold sweat.

A **compound sentence** contains two or more simple sentences (independent clauses) that have been joined together. For example:

> Pam saw the shark and she screamed.
> I heard Pam's scream, but I could not see what had frightened her.

Compound sentences are usually held together by conjunctions. The words *and* and *but* in the sentences above are examples of coordinating conjunctions. For more information about conjunctions, see the **Just for Fun!** section on the next page.

A **compound-complex sentence** contains at least two independent clauses and one dependent clause. For example:

> Ashley wanted an eagle for her birthday, but because eagles are an endangered species, her parents bought her a turkey instead.
>
> Although she wasn't crazy about turkeys, Ashley took the bird under her wing, and it became her new best friend.

Sentences may also be classified based upon their content and purpose. **Declarative sentences** give information and end in periods. For example:

> This is a declarative sentence.
> Indian elephants have smaller ears than African elephants.

Exclamatory sentences communicate strong emotion or surprise and end with exclamation points. For example:

> The yak thief is back in town!
> My neighbor's yak is missing!

Notes:

Interrogative sentences ask questions and always end with question marks. For example:

> Did you see Bo's new suspenders?
> Did you know that Bo's favorite sport is shuffleboard?

In A Nutshell:

A **simple sentence** contains a single independent clause.

A **complex sentence** contains an independent and a dependent clause.

A **compound sentence** contains two or more simple sentences.

A **compound-complex** sentence contains at least two independent clauses and one dependent clause.

Declarative sentences give information and end in periods.

Exclamatory sentences communicate strong emotion or surprise and end with exclamation points.

Interrogative sentences ask questions and always end with question marks.

Just for Fun!

Conjunctions are the words that hold sentences together. In the same way that a mechanic needs nuts and bolts to hold his machinery together, so our sentences need certain words to hold them together. Conjunctions are just those kinds of words.

More than that, though, conjunctions show the logical connections between words or groups of words. By paying attention to conjunctions, you can usually see the logical relations between sentences and parts of sentences. For example:

And says that two or more things belong together.

> *Seth threw a ball, and Maggie caught it.*

But shows a contrast between two or more things.

> *Seth threw a ball, but Maggie dropped it.*

Or says that only one of two different things is true.

> *I will go to the grocery store, or I will go to the movies.*

So says that one thing is true because something else is true.

> *I will go to the grocery store, so I will have food to eat tomorrow.*

A **coordinating conjunction** is a special type of conjunction that connects words, phrases, or clauses when the words, phrases, or clauses are of equal importance. There are seven coordinating conjunctions that can be memorized by simply remembering: **FANBOYS**.

For (Wayne must be flying his kite, *for* it is the first windy day in weeks.)
And (peas *and* carrots)
Nor (neither rain *nor* snow)
But (I love peas, *but* I do not care for carrots.)
Or (this *or* that)
Yet (Ashley loves her new turkey, *yet* it is not exactly the present she had hoped for.)
So (Jason and Jennifer are hungry for Italian food, *so* they are heading to Little Italy.)

If you memorize the coordinating conjunctions, you'll know that any other conjunctions you see will be subordinating conjunctions that begin dependent clauses. In addition to holding simple sentences together to form compound sentences, coordinating conjunctions can also hold two or more nouns or verbs together. For example:

> Sam I Am hates green eggs *and* ham, but he eats them.
> Beth *and* Ann ran to the store.

Finally, don't forget that independent clauses can also begin with a coordinating conjunction. They may seem like dependent clauses, since you'll need to know the context to understand them. For example, if you see a sentence that begins, "And _____," you will realize something came before. And you will probably want to know what it was. But, of course, it is acceptable to begin a simple sentence with *and*, *or*, or *but*.

Application:

Choose several activities to do over the course of the week to reinforce what you've taught your children about types of sentences:

☐ It will behoove you to spend some extra time with your **Grammar Rock DVD** this week. First, review **The Tale Of Mr. Morton** to brush up on subjects and predicates, the basics of sentences. Then, take another look at **Conjunction Junction** and keep an eye open for coordinating conjunctions. Finally, watch **Interjections!** to learn more about exclamatory sentences.

☐ Play the **End That Sentence!** game from **Lesson 3: Sentences**. If you still have them, use the set of punctuation flashcards you made previously. If you don't have them any more, just make another set as follows. Using three 3X5 cards, write the punctuation marks on them (period, question mark, and exclamation point). Then make up some silly sentences and say them to your children. When you're done saying each sentence, have your children hold up the flashcard with the proper punctuation for the sentence. In addition, ask them to tell you what type of sentence corresponds to that punctuation mark (declarative, exclamatory, or interrogative). Be sure to incorporate a mixture of the different types of sentences.

☐ Challenge your children to so some more **Editing** of their recent work. Unless they're advanced writers, your children have probably been using mostly simple sentences. However, good writers know that their readers enjoy it when they use a variety of different types of sentences. Ask your children to analyze their recent work to determine what types of sentences they've been using. Encourage them to add variety by using several different types of sentences. Feel free to help them along. Suggest that they combine two or more short sentences into one compound sentence. Or change shorter sentences into dependent clauses to add to other sentences.

Notes:

Notes:

☐ Try your hand at **Sentence Typing** on **Side A** of the **Lesson 20: Types of Sentences** **Student Activity Sheet**. Ask your children to read the sentences in the chart to determine whether they are simple, complex, compound, or compound-complex. Then have them put an "X" in the appropriate column following each sentence.

☐ Is it a **.** **or !** **or ?** Ask your children to read the sentences in the chart on **Side B** of the **Lesson 20: Types of Sentences** **Student Activity Sheet** to determine whether they are declarative, exclamatory, or interrogative. Then have them put an "X" in the appropriate column following each sentence.

Answer Key

Side A: Sentence Typing

1. Simple
2. Complex
3. Compound
4. Compound-Complex
5. Compound
6. Simple
7. Compound-Complex
8. Complex
9. Simple
10. Compound
11. Complex
12. Compound-Complex

Side B: . or ! or ?

1. Exclamatory
2. Interrogative
3. Declarative
4. Declarative
5. Exclamatory
6. Interrogative
7. Exclamatory
8. Declarative
9. Interrogative
10. Declarative
11. Exclamatory
12. Interrogative

Lesson 21: Paragraphs

> **P**ARAGRAPH: A paragraph is a distinct portion of written or printed matter dealing with a particular idea, usually beginning with an indentation on a new line.

Teaching Instruction:

A **paragraph** is a group of sentences. But it's not just any old group of sentences. The sentences in a paragraph convey a common idea or hold together in a logical manner. For example:

> Although Duane desperately wanted his computer fixed, Ryan decided that the problem was best ignored. Frustrated, but resigned, Duane continued his work. Unfortunately, the problem continued to rear its head. It would not be ignored!

A paragraph may consist of just a couple of sentences or hundreds of sentences. Paragraphs are set apart from one another either by placing extra space between them (like the paragraphs on this page) or by indenting the first line of each paragraph by four or five spaces like this:

> Jack really missed off-roading. Even though he loved his minivan, he longed for the days when he could attack a backwoods trail and see sights reserved for the truly adventurous. Perhaps his wife would buy him a new four-wheel-drive vehicle for his birthday. What a gift that would be!

Logically, a paragraph should be a set of sentences about the same subject. To understand how each paragraph in an essay or book or story can have its own topic that holds the sentences together, we must talk about topic sentences.

A **topic sentence** is usually found at the beginning of each new paragraph, identifying that paragraph's topic. Not all paragraphs have topic sentences, but they should be used in every persuasive paragraph and every paragraph of a formal essay.

Although it introduces the subject of the paragraph, a topic sentence doesn't necessarily knock you over the head and scream *this is what this paragraph is about!* Instead, it whispers what the paragraph is about; it gives you hints. Here are some examples:

> In first grade, Seth learned some of the harsh realities of life. More people should know how to administer first aid.

Using these examples, think about the paragraphs they introduce. *In first grade, Seth learned some of the harsh realities of life.* What is this paragraph going to be about? You would probably expect to find a list of lessons about life that Seth learned in first grade. Maybe it will contain some stories about the circumstances and experiences by which he learned his lessons. *More people should know how to administer first aid.* This paragraph probably has to do with first aid, why it is important, and/or the reasons why more people should learn how to administer it.

Notes:

_____

_____

_____

_____

_____

_____

_____

_____

_____

_____

_____

_____

_____

_____

_____

_____

_____

_____

_____

_____

_____

_____

_____

_____

_____

In A Nutshell:

A **paragraph** is a group of sentences that convey a common idea or hold together in a logical manner.

A **topic sentence** is usually found at the beginning of each new paragraph, identifying that paragraph's topic.

Application:

Choose several activities to do over the course of the week to reinforce what you've taught your children about paragraphs:

☐ Review any of the songs we've covered already on your _Grammar Rock_ DVD.

☐ As you read with your children throughout the week, play **Point Out the Paragraph**. Ask your children to identify paragraphs. Point out the various features of paragraphs: topic sentences, indentations, etc. Show them short paragraphs and long paragraphs. Discuss how the sentences in the paragraphs relate to the same subject.

☐ Have your children **Finish the Paragraph** on **Side A** of the **Lesson 21: Paragraphs Student Activity Sheet**. We've provided six possible topic sentences. Read through them with your children and ask them to pick their favorite. They should then use that topic sentence as the first sentence of their own original paragraph. On the lines provided, ask them to write two to four additional sentences that they think would logically come after their chosen topic sentence in a paragraph.

☐ Challenge your children to fix our **Humpty Dumpty Paragraph** on **Side B** of the **Lesson 21: Paragraphs Student Activity Sheet**. Explain to them that we wrote a great paragraph and hung it on the wall. But it fell down and broke into a bunch of sentences! All the sentences were scattered and they got mixed up with some other sentences that were lying on the floor. We need your children's help to put our paragraph back together. Ask them to read all the sentences in the chart and decide which sentences should go together in our paragraph. Hint: Only five of the sentences belong in our paragraph. When they've figured out which sentences belong in our paragraph, have them put them in an order that makes sense and then write the paragraph on the lines below the chart.

Answer Key

Side A: Finish the Paragraph

Answers will vary.

_____

Side B: Humpty Dumpty Paragraph

Answers will vary. Here is a possible answer:

Fall is my favorite time of year. I love to see the first hints of the coming winter. Falling leaves carpet the ground in a kaleidoscope of color. The brisk air is perfect for the start of football season. It's the perfect time to enjoy the outdoors for a few final weeks before settling in for the long wait for spring.

Lesson 22: Expository Paragraphs

> EXPOSITORY PARAGRAPH: An expository paragraph is a paragraph that serves to expound, set forth, or explain something.

Teaching Instruction:

An **expository paragraph** explains something; it *exposes* the meaning of something or the reason why. An expository paragraph is meant to convey information or to help the reader's understanding. As when we dissect an animal, peeling back its skin, muscles and bones to reveal what lies beneath and inside, so the expository paragraph peels back and exposes what is inside a topic of discussion. Here is an example of an expository paragraph:

> Natural disasters often result in uncommon scientific collaborations. For example, seismologists are geophysics specialists who study earthquakes. Oceanographers, on the other hand, study the many features of oceans. While these experts in land and sea would normally have little interaction, an undersea earthquake that causes a tsunami—a giant tidal wave—will force them to combine their expertise in order to understand the events.

Expository paragraphs are distinct from, though they may contain elements of, persuasive, narrative, or descriptive paragraphs. Even if it is telling a story or describing something, an expository paragraph's primary purpose is explanation.

Encyclopedia articles are almost always made up of purely expository paragraphs. But you'll find expository paragraphs elsewhere as well: in fiction, you may find that the author has a character *think something through* so that you understand what you (and the character) did not understand before.

In non-fiction books, most authors who expose you to new information want to do more than merely teach you something new. They want to convince you that they are correct about some matter. If a paragraph goes beyond merely informing and is obviously written to convince you about a matter, it is called a persuasive paragraph. We'll take an in-depth look at persuasive paragraphs in the next lesson.

In A Nutshell:

An **expository paragraph** explains something; it *exposes* the meaning of something or the reason why. An expository paragraph is meant to convey information or to help the reader's understanding.

Application:

Choose several activities to do over the course of the week to reinforce what you've taught your children about expository paragraphs:

☐ Review any of the songs we've covered already on your ***Grammar Rock*** DVD.

☐ Do some **Encyclopedia Research**. Crack open the old encyclopedia, or go to an online encyclopedia, such as those that can be found at **www.wikipedia.org**, **www.encyclopedia.com**, or elsewhere on the Internet. Pick out some subjects that interest your children. Let them read the encyclopedia articles about these subjects and, as they read, explain to them how the paragraphs convey information to help the reader's understanding. Reinforce their understanding of what an expository paragraph is in this way.

☐ Send your children on a wild **Paragraph Hunt**. Give them a magazine (for this particular exercise, good magazines would include history magazines or science magazines such as *Popular Mechanics* or *National Geographic*) and ask them to find three good examples of expository paragraphs. Remind them of what an expository paragraph is and give them some hints about where to look for them.

☐ Tell us **Why, Oh Why?** on **Side A** of the <u>**Lesson 22: Expository Paragraphs**</u> **Student Activity Sheet**. We're in a curious mood and want to know why certain things are the way they are. Have your children pick one of the questions in the chart and do some quick encyclopedia or Internet research on it. Don't let them spend more than 15 minutes or so finding the "quick" answer to the question. Then ask them to write a good expository paragraph explaining the answer to the question.

☐ Challenge your children to write a creative expository paragraph about **The XJ-9** on **Side B** of the <u>**Lesson 22: Expository Paragraphs**</u> **Student Activity Sheet.** Your children probably think that expository paragraphs don't leave much room for creativity. Well, most of the time that's true. Expository paragraphs are all about the facts, ma'am. But we're going to give them a rare chance here. We want them to write an expository paragraph about the XJ-9, the first space-age whatchamacallit that can …well, make your children tell us what it can do! Have them write an expository paragraph about the XJ-9. Explain it to us. Why and how does it do what it does? They have no choice but to be creative now. Feel free to give them all the help they need on this one.

Answer Key

Side A: Why, Oh Why?

Answers will vary.

Side B: The XJ-9

Answers will vary.

Lesson 23: Persuasuve Paragraphs

> PERSUASIVE PARAGRAPH: A persuasive paragraph is a paragraph intended or having the power to induce action or belief.

Teaching Instruction:

A **persuasive paragraph** seeks to convince or persuade the reader that something is true or that a particular viewpoint is preferred. For example, in non-fiction books, most authors who expose you to new information want to convince you that they are correct about some matter. Here is an example of a persuasive paragraph:

> Our state should have a mandatory seat belt law. Using seat belts has proven to be a powerful factor in reducing traffic-related fatalities and injuries. Plus, it is a sad, but proven fact that some people will simply not do certain things in their best interest unless forced to do so.

What do you think? Are you persuaded? Can you see why this paragraph is considered a persuasive paragraph? Often the topic sentence will provide the necessary clues: *Our state should have a mandatory seat belt law.* The use of the word *should* is a good indicator that the author is trying to persuade the reader.

Persuasive paragraphs are different from—although they may look a little like—narrative, expository, or descriptive paragraphs. Keep in mind that it can be tough to persuade someone with only one paragraph. Paragraphs are usually parts of longer persuasive works, such as essays, articles, or books, though. So the important thing to remember is that persuasive paragraphs are obviously meant to *persuade* rather than merely *explain* or *expose*.

In A Nutshell:

Persuasive paragraphs seek to convince or persuade the reader that something is true or that a particular viewpoint is preferred.

Application:

Choose several activities to do over the course of the week to reinforce what you've taught your children about persuasive paragraphs:

☐ Review any of the songs we've covered already on your *Grammar Rock* **DVD**.

☐ Send your children on another **Paragraph Hunt**. Give them a magazine or a newspaper (for this particular exercise, good sources would include news magazines or newspapers with opinion pages/sections) and ask them to find three good examples of persuasive paragraphs. Remind them of what a persuasive paragraph is and give them some hints about where to look for them. As a challenge, ask them to evaluate the paragraphs. Does the author do a good job of persuading the reader?

☐ Help your children hone their **Powers of Persuasion** this week. If your children are like most, they probably make a few requests of you on a daily basis. This week, make your children lobby on behalf of themselves when they make a request. If they ask for a snack, respond with, "Persuade me that letting you have a snack is a good idea. Convince me that it won't ruin your dinner." If they request some of your time to play a game with them, ask them to give you three good reasons why your time is best spent playing a game with them, rather than doing laundry, dishes, or any of those other all-important chores. Practicing persuasion in this way will benefit your children when they begin to practice writing persuasive paragraphs.

☐ Do your children think they're pretty persuasive writers? Well, here's their chance to **Convince Me!** on **Side A** of the <u>**Lesson 23: Persuasive Paragraphs**</u> **Student Activity Sheet.** We have listed five topic sentences. Ask your children to read through them and choose the one for which they believe they can make the best case. Then have them write a persuasive paragraph based upon their chosen topic sentence. If they don't like any of our topic sentences, feel free to let them make up their own topic sentence. Just encourage them to work hard to put together a good paragraph that persuades the reader that their opinion or viewpoint is correct.

☐ Do your children have the **#1 Mom or Dad**? We'll bet you think they do! And we'll bet your children do too. Ask them to persuade us that you're really #1 on **Side B** of the <u>**Lesson 23: Persuasive Paragraphs**</u> **Student Activity Sheet**. Moms and dads are the greatest—for many reasons. What reasons do your children have? Most kids feel like their particular moms and dads are the greatest, though, so your children are going to have to be pretty persuasive to make their readers believe that *their* mom or dad really is the tops. Ask them to write a persuasive paragraph to convince their readers that they really do have the #1 mom or dad in the universe. And you might also want to subtly remind them that this particular assignment can score them big points with their teacher!

Answer Key

Side A: Convince Me

Answers will vary.

Side B: #1 Mom or Dad

Answers will vary.

Lesson 24: Descriptive Paragraphs

> **D**ESCRIPTIVE PARAGRAPH: A descriptive paragraph is a paragraph serving to describe or inform or characterized by description.

Teaching Instruction:

A **descriptive paragraph** is dedicated primarily to describing something. Descriptive paragraphs paint a clear picture of a person, place, thing, or idea—how it looks, smells, sounds, tastes, and/or feels. Here is an example of a descriptive paragraph:

> The turkey clucked in excitement as it escaped from the box. It was the most unique bird Ashley had ever seen. Its long, silky feathers of every color glistened in the light like a sunset. Its sparkling eyes somehow knew her already. As it pranced around the room, it made a peculiar sound that Ashley knew meant Thanksgiving would never be the same again.

Do you have a picture of the turkey in your mind? Can you see it prancing? What does its clucking sound like? These types of details based upon our senses—seeing, smelling, tasting, hearing, and feeling—give descriptive paragraphs their unique character and powerful impact.

Descriptive paragraphs are different from—although though they may look a little like—persuasive, expository, or narrative paragraphs. You will find descriptive paragraphs in just about any written work, though they are more common in historical works and works of fiction.

In A Nutshell:

Descriptive paragraphs paint a clear picture of a person, place, thing, or idea—how it looks, smells, sounds, tastes, and/or feels.

Application:

Choose several activities to do over the course of the week to reinforce what you've taught your children about descriptive paragraphs:

☐ Review any of the songs we've covered already on your *Grammar Rock* DVD.

☐ Play a guessing game with your children based upon their **Five Senses**. Start with one of the senses, such as smell, and pretend that you smell something. It can be good or bad. It can be something you can smell at that moment or something completely made up. It's up to you. Give your children details about that smell. Describe it. Then have them guess what it is you smell. Is it bacon frying? Is it potpourri on the end table? Is it sweaty camels after a long trek through the desert? Phew! We hope not! Go through each of the senses and take turns so you let your children be the smeller, or the seer, or the hearer, or the feeler, or the taster. As you play, explain to your children that such details based upon our senses are what make descriptive paragraphs so special. Encouraging to think along these lines will help them be more creative when they practice writing descriptive paragraphs.

☐ Send your children on a **Descriptive Paragraph Hunt**. Give them a magazine or a book (for this particular exercise, good sources would include biographical magazines like People, cooking magazines, or popular fiction books) and ask them to find three good examples of descriptive paragraphs. Remind them of what a descriptive paragraph is and give them some hints about where to look for them.

☐ Challenge your children to **Make It Real** on **Side A** of the **Lesson 24: Descriptive Paragraphs** Student Activity Sheet. We have listed five things for your children to pick from. Ask them to pick one and write a descriptive paragraph about it. If they don't like our suggestions, feel free to allow them to pick something on their own. Just make sure they write a vivid, detailed descriptive paragraph that leaves nothing to the imagination. Can they touch on all five senses in their paragraph? Make these rather nondescript things real for your their readers.

☐ Do your children have a **Favorite Place**? On the lines on **Side B** of the **Lesson 24: Descriptive Paragraphs** Student Activity Sheet, ask them to write a descriptive paragraph that brings their favorite place to life for the reader. Where is it? What does it look like? Does it have a particularly comforting smell? What can you hear when you're there? Are there any special feelings or tastes that you associate with it? Asking them these types of questions based upon their five senses will help your children think of the details that will make their descriptive paragraph sing.

Answer Key

Side A: Make It Real

Answers will vary.

Side B: Favorite Place

Answers will vary.

Lesson 25: Narrative Paragraphs

> **N**ARRATIVE PARAGRAPH: A narrative paragraph is a paragraph consisting of or characterized by the telling of a story.

Teaching Instruction:

A **narrative paragraph** tells a story; it describes an event, feeling or experience in story form or in the order the details of the event happened. Narrative paragraphs are often used to describe what a person does over a period of time. Transition words that provide time clues, such as yesterday, after, then, later, etc., are often a good indication that you're reading a narrative paragraph. Here is an example of a narrative paragraph:

> Yesterday evening Martha completed all of her errands. After leaving her office, she stopped at the spa for a quick sea kelp eye treatment. Then she hurried to the organic food store to pick up a pound of tofu for dinner. Later she swung by the dry cleaners to retrieve her black cocktail dress she intended to wear to her company's Christmas party.

Did you notice the transition words that provided time clues about the order of Martha's errands? Do you see how this paragraph *narrates* the events of Martha's evening? After reading this paragraph, you have a good idea of what happened over the course of Martha's evening.

Narrative paragraphs are different from—although though they may look a little like—persuasive, expository, or descriptive paragraphs. Unlike the other types of paragraphs, narrative paragraphs focus on *what happened*. You will find narrative paragraphs in any written work that relates a story of any kind or tells what happened to someone or something.

In A Nutshell:

A **narrative paragraph** tells a story; it describes an event, feeling or experience in story form or in the order the details of the event happened.

Application:

Choose several activities to do over the course of the week to reinforce what you've taught your children about narrative paragraphs:

☐ Review any of the songs we've covered already on your ***Grammar Rock*** DVD.

☐ Send your children on a **Narrative Paragraph Hunt**. Ask them to pick out their favorite book that they've read recently and find three good examples of narrative paragraphs. Remind them of what a narrative paragraph is and give them some hints about where to look for them. Encourage them to look for transition words that provide time clues about the chronological order of the events that take place.

☐ Have some fun this week **Telling Stories**. Storytelling is a grand tradition in most, if not all, cultures around the world. Spinning a yarn is a treasured pastime that has served a key role in passing down memories and family heritage for thousands of years. All stories feature mainly narrative paragraphs, so telling stories with your children will reinforce what you've taught them about narrative paragraphs. Tell your children stories about when you were a child, about their relatives, about the history of your state, about anything you want! Also encourage your children to tell you stories about themselves, their friends, and their own favorite family memories. Cherish this special time together—it's what homeschooling is all about!

☐ What did your children do **Last Night**? Ask them to write a narrative paragraph that tells the story of what they did last night on **Side A** of the **Lesson 25: Narrative Paragraphs** Student Activity Sheet. Help them remember what they did. Was it homework? Did they watch television? Play with a friend? Take a bath? Walk the dog? Climb a mountain? Save the planet from a meteor the size of Texas? Whatever they did, we want to know about it. It doesn't have to be exciting; it just has to be what really happened. Remind them to use transition words that will give their readers clear time clues about what occurred when.

☐ Challenge your children to put together the **Story Puzzle** on **Side B** of the **Lesson 25: Narrative Paragraphs** Student Activity Sheet. We have listed five things that happened to Molly Moose and Ben Beaver on their way home yesterday after school. Ask your children to read through them and put them in an order that they think makes sense. Then have them weave them together into a narrative paragraph that tells the exciting story of what happened to Molly and Ben yesterday afternoon.

Answer Key

Side A: Last Night

Answers will vary.

Side B: Story Puzzle

Answers will vary.

Lesson 26: Prefixes & Suffixes

> **P**REFIX: A prefix is a letter combination attached to the front of a word to produce a derivative word or an inflected form.
>
> **S**UFFIX: A suffix is a letter combination added to the end of a word or stem, serving to form a new word or functioning as an inflectional ending.

Teaching Instruction:

Many words come in different forms. For example:

want, wants, wanting, wanted, unwanted
blink, blinks, blinking, unblinking, blinked

Each word, though, has a root or core meaning. In the examples above, what is the root or core meaning? (*want* and *blink*) These words that represent the root or core meaning are called **root words**.

As you saw above, we can add parts—called prefixes and/or suffixes—to the root word to change its meaning. Here are the same examples with the prefixes and suffixes italicized:

want, want*s*, want*ing*, want*ed*, *un*want*ed*
blink, blink*s*, blink*ing*, *un*blink*ing*, blink*ed*

A **prefix** is a letter combination added to the beginning of a root word to change its meaning. Remember: Prefixes go before (pre) the root word. For example:

Un-, when added to a root word, reverses its meaning. Someone can *do* something, and someone else can *undo* it. One person may say an idea is *important*, and someone else may say it's *unimportant*.

Im- has a similar effect. One person may think that something is *possible*, but another may believe it's *impossible*.

A **suffix** is a letter combination added to the end of a root word to change its meaning. For example:

Book is a root word. If you add the suffix -s to it, it becomes *books*. What happened? Adding the suffix *-s* changes the meaning from singular to plural. Similarly, adding the suffix *-ed* to the end of the root word *want* changes it from present tense to past tense (*wanted*).

In A Nutshell:

Prefixes are letter combinations added to the beginning of root words to change their meaning.

Suffixes are letter combinations added to the end of root words to change their meaning.

The words to which prefixes and/or suffixes are added and that represent the root or core meaning are called **root words**.

Application:

Choose several activities to do over the course of the week to reinforce what you've taught your children about prefixes and suffixes:

☐ Review any of the songs we've covered already on your **Grammar Rock** DVD.

Notes:

☐ Play **Prefix/Suffix Spotter** as you read with your children this week. Pick out a particular page and then, as you read, ask your children to point out all of the words that have prefixes and suffixes. Can they figure out what the root words are? Discuss with them how the prefixes and/or suffixes change the meaning of the root words. Do they make them plural? Change the verb tense? Negate the meaning? Feel free to look up the words in a dictionary if you need help figuring out the meaning of the prefixes and/or suffixes.

☐ Challenge your children to engage in some **Word Building** on **Side A** of the <u>**Lesson 26: Prefixes & Suffixes**</u> **Student Activity Sheet**. How many new words can they make out of the root words listed? Ask them to add prefixes and/or suffixes to the root words and write the new words in the column to the right. Give them some help if they get stuck on any of the words. Make sure they think of at least three new words for each root word.

☐ Ask your children to **Uncover the Root** on **Side B** of the <u>**Lesson 26:**</u> <u>**Prefixes & Suffixes**</u> **Student Activity Sheet**. Have them analyze the words in the left column. Can they remove the prefixes and/or suffixes to uncover the root word? When they figure it out, ask them to write the root word in the column on the right. Feel free to help them if they get stuck on any word.

Answer Key

Side A Word Building

Answers will vary.
Possible answers include:

1. acts, acting, acted, react, reacted
2. travels, traveling, traveled
3. quieted, quietly, quietness
4. members, remember, remembered,
5. sprayed, sprayer, spraying
6. placing, placed, replace, replaced
7. flaming, inflamed, flames
8. unjust, justly, adjust, adjusting
9. fairly, unfair, unfairly, fairness
10. smiley, smiler, smilingly, smiled

Side B Uncover the Root

1. probable
2. thank
3. like
4. hair
5. desire
6. gust
7. tract
8. peril
9. faith
10. trick

Lesson 27: Commas

> **C**OMMA: A comma is a mark of punctuation used for indicating a division in a sentence, as in setting off a word, phrase, or clause. It is also used to separate items in a list, to mark off thousands in numerals, and to separate types of information in bibliographic and other data.

Teaching Instruction:

Notes:

The **comma** (,) may just be the most versatile mark of punctuation. Among its many uses, one of the most prominent is as a separator, helping to add clarity to a sentence. There are so many uses of commas that we can't list them all here. However, here are some examples of the most common uses of the comma:

Between independent clauses that are joined by a coordinating conjunction:

> I went to the grocery store, but my best friend went to the hockey game.

To separate items in a series:

> I went to the grocery store to buy apples, soda, bread, and laundry detergent.

Note: Always separate three or more items in a list by using commas between them. However, do not use commas between the members of a series composed of only two items—unless the comma is necessary for clarity's sake. If the last item in a list is preceded by the word *and*, you may, but you don't have to, place a comma between the next-to-last item in the list and the word *and*. For example, both of these examples are correct:

> Please buy peanut butter, jelly, bread, graham crackers, and milk.

> Please buy peanut butter, jelly, bread, graham crackers and milk.

To separate nonrestrictive clauses from the rest of the sentence:

> The grocery store, which was built last year, is always busy on Saturdays.

To separate multiple adjectives:

> It was an exciting, busy day at the grocery store.

After introductory phrases or clauses:

> After a hard day of work, I like to go grocery shopping.

To set off dates or items in addresses:

> On July 2, 1997, I went to the grocery store located at 7 Lucky Drive, Anytown, Colorado 54321.

To clarify large numbers:

> 1,000 apples or 1,000,000 oranges

To separate contrasted or parenthetical information:

> Sue, not Judy, is the guilty one.

To set off explanatory phrases or appositives:

> Samson, my Weimaraner puppy, is fond of perpetual motion.

To set off dialogue and nouns of direct address:

> "Thad, put the spatula in the dishwasher," said Joan.

To set off interjections or interruptions:

> Hey, stop that! In my opinion, well, you just shouldn't be doing that.

To set off titles or initials:

> John F. Kennedy, Jr., started *George* magazine.

To clarify otherwise confusing text:

> What the production department does, does change the shipping department's work schedule.

In A Nutshell:

The **comma** (,) is one of the most versatile marks of punctuation. Among its many uses, one of the most prominent is as a separator, helping to add clarity to a sentence.

Application:

Choose several activities to do over the course of the week to reinforce what you've taught your children about commas:

☐ Review **Conjunction Junction and Interjections!** on your **Grammar Rock DVD**. Pay particular attention to how commas are used in these lessons.

☐ Encourage your children to do some more **Editing** of their recent work. Have they been using commas? If so, have they been using them correctly? Can your children rewrite any of their sentences to make them clearer by using commas?

☐ As you read aloud with your children this week, **Point Out the Commas** and discuss how they're being used in the sentences you read. Are they used to clarify large numbers? To set off introductory phrases or appositives? To separate the members of a series? Talk to your children about how the commas are used to make the sentences clearer and easier to understand. For fun, try removing some of the commas and see how confusing some sentences can get!

☐ Challenge your children to figure out **Where, Oh Where, Do the Commas Go?** on **Side A** of the **Lesson 27: Commas** Student Activity Sheet. We wrote a bunch of sentences to help show your children how commas are used. Then someone—we won't say who—bumped the page and all the commas fell right out of our sentences. It was a disaster! At least we were able to get them all swept up again. Can your children help us put them all back in our sentences? Ask them to read our sentences and put commas back in where they're needed. Feel free to give them some help if they need it.

□ We have **Too Many Commas!** on **Side B** of the <u>**Lesson 27: Commas**</u> **Student Activity Sheet**. What is going on here? Where did all of these extra commas come from? When we wrote these sentences, we know we used commas in only the correct places. We turn our backs for one second and—bam!—commas everywhere! Please ask your children to help us fix these sentences by marking out all of the commas that don't belong.

Answer Key

Side A: Where, Oh Where, Do the Commas Go?

1. Jimmy, can you please tell Fay to pick up the rubber bands around her desk?
2. Loretta saw ducks, geese, and pigeons at the park.
3. Karleen likes roast beef, but Mike prefers ham.
4. C.J. Binstrap, Sr., began working on the website on October 31, 2006.
5. Amber looked at the sky and thought there must be 1,000,000 stars up there.
6. Ronda, Brazil's most famous tour guide, drove the guests to the hotel.
7. Once upon a time, a frog tried to teach kids how to tell time.
8. Your mom lives at 8042 S. Grant Way, Littleton, Colorado 80122.
9. Gary's children, Harry, Barry, Larry, and Ned, love to torment their father.
10. Melinda was lucky to have witnessed such a beautiful, exciting spectacle.
11. Colleen, the newest member of the department, suffered through her initiation.
12. The deli on the corner, which opened yesterday, was crowded during lunch.

Side B: Too Many Commas!

1. The baby beaver was born on December 8, 2006.
2. Frank F. Fickle felt funny fishing for freshwater flounder.
3. Marjorie's favorite lunch was tuna and ice cream.
4. The secret meeting took place at 2 Mystery Lane, Peso, Texas 12345.
5. Maggie's dog was really big and brown.
6. The janitor cleaned the floors after midnight.
7. Aly played guitar and sang at the dance.
8. Reilly had a crush on Seth, her favorite boy in the class.
9. Luke, the most brilliant director in Hollywood, drives a red truck.
10. Amy saves money each month by buying only bread and rice.
11. Justin, the fiercest ninja fighter at camp, sprained his ankle.
12. Dave's mother-in-law scolded him for lying and cheating.

Lesson 28: Analogies

> ANALOGY: An analogy is a comparison between two things that are similar in some way, often used to help explain something or make it easier to understand.

Teaching Instruction:

An **analogy** compares two (or more) things that are similar in some important way in order to help explain something or make something easier to understand. Although the items compared may otherwise be dissimilar, analogies are used to suggest that because they are similar in a certain way they are also similar in some further way. Here is an example:

> Phil hates receiving unsolicited "spam" e-mail because deleting it from his inbox wastes so much time. He insists there must be some solution to this problem on the horizon! Of course, he also used to think that, by now, he wouldn't need to continually pitch the "junk" mail that accumulates in his mailbox on a daily basis.

The analogy in this paragraph suggests that "spam" e-mail, like postal "junk" mail, may be here to stay.

A **simile** is a special type of analogy that compares two things that are not obviously similar and suggests there are similarities. Similes use the words *like* or *as*. Here are some examples of similes:

> Flash was fast *as lightning.*
> The seven penguins were *like princesses.*

Similes help readers to understand better what an author is talking about. They help us form pictures in our minds. Authors also use similes to cause readers to *think more deeply* about what is being written.

A **metaphor** is a special type of analogy that compares two different things using imaginative phrases to make them seem the same when they are really different. Instead of being directly compared, though, one thing is actually said *to be* another. In each case, the statement is not literally true, but it communicates something that is true in a powerful way. The reader is expected to interpret what the truth is. Here are some examples of metaphors:

> Fran *is ice.*
> Jake *was a rock.*

Is Fran frozen in water? No, but the metaphor tells the reader she is cold. Likewise, is Jake an actual rock? No, but the metaphor tells the reader his muscles are solid and hard.

As you can see, a metaphor compares two things, but doesn't tell us it is making a comparison. We have to figure that out on our own.

In A Nutshell:

An **analogy** compares things that are similar in some important way in order to help explain something or make something easier to understand.

A **simile** is a special type of analogy using the words *like* or *as*.

A **metaphor** is a special type of analogy in which one thing is actually said *to be* another.

Notes:

Notes:

Application:

Choose several activities to do over the course of the week to reinforce what you've taught your children about analogies:

☐ To develop great analogies, one must think in descriptive terms. Review **Unpack Your Adjectives** and **Lolly, Lolly, Lolly, Get Your Adverbs Here** on your **Grammar Rock** DVD to help get your children in a descriptive frame of mind.

☐ Play a game of **Simile Word Association**. Think of a list of at least 10 adjectives. Then say each adjective to your children and ask them to respond with the first simile that comes to mind. For example, you say "red" and they say "as an apple" or "like a cherry." Or you say "mad" and they say "as a wet hen." Challenge your children to answer as quickly as possible with the first simile that comes to mind. Just make sure they use *like* or *as*.

☐ Help us solve the **Simile Snafu** on **Side A** of the **Lesson 28: Analogies Student Activity Sheet**. We wrote some really funny sentences using similes the other day. We set them aside, and when we got them out today, the similes were all gone! Can your children help us recreate these funny sentences by filling in the blanks with some creative similes of their own?

☐ Challenge your children to create some **Marvelous Metaphors** on **Side B** of the **Lesson 28: Analogies** Student Activity Sheet. Creative metaphors enliven any piece of writing. They help authors paint a vivid tableau for their readers. Can your children help us finish the sentences we started by filling in the blanks in a way that will create some marvelous metaphors?

Answer Key

Side A: Simile Snafu

Answers will vary.

Side B: Marvelous Metaphors

Answers will vary.

Lesson 29: Quotations

> QUOTATION: A quotation is a piece of speech or writing repeated or copied exactly as spoken or written.

Teaching Instruction:

Occasionally authors want to copy what someone else said or wrote exactly as it was spoken or written. When they do so, they create a **quotation**. But how will readers know that the quoted words were spoken or written by someone else? To set off a quotation, authors use quotation marks.

Quotation marks (" ") are marks of punctuation used to indicate *exactly* what someone else said or wrote. Quotation marks are placed immediately before and after what was said. For example:

Maggie said, "Give me the ball, Seth."

If the words aren't being quoted exactly as they were spoken, your quotation is called an **indirect quotation** and it should not be placed inside quotation marks. For example:

Maggie asked Seth to give her the ball.

A regular quotation is enclosed within regular (double) quotation marks (" "). If the person being quoted then quotes someone else, the quote he is quoting is enclosed within single quotation marks (' '). If this quote-within-a-quote should happen also to include a quote, this third quote-within-a-quote-within-a-quote will be enclosed within double quotes once more, and so the pattern would continue. For example:

Judy said, "Your mom said to come home now."
Judy said, "Your mom said, 'Come home now.'"
Judy said, "Your mom said, 'I said, "Come home now."'"

Quotation marks are also used for titles of certain works and to set off special words or phrases. For example:

"Like A Rolling Stone" (song title)
Pam is not allowed to use the phrase "bling bling" around her
   teenage daughter.

Ending punctuation (commas, periods, question marks, etc.) should usually be placed inside (before) the closing quotation mark. For example:

"Come to the baseball game," he said.
"You'll have a great time."

If the quotation is a question, the question mark should come inside the closing quotation mark. If, however, the quotation itself is not a question, but you are asking a question about the quotation, then the question mark is placed outside of the quotation mark.

"Am I dreaming?"
Did she really hear him say "You must have been dreaming"?

Notes:

Similarly, with exclamation points, if the quotation itself is an exclamation, then the exclamation point is placed inside the final quotation mark. If the quotation is *not* an exclamation, but you are exclaiming about the quotation, then the exclamation point should come outside the quote. For example:

"You are amazing!"
Imagine, he couldn't remember her saying "You are amazing"!

The phrase that indicates who said whatever it is you're quoting—Daren said, Jenny yelled, etc.—is called the **attribution**. An attribution can be placed before, in the middle of, or after the quotation. When the attribution is before the quotation, identify who is being quoted, follow that with a comma, and then begin the quotation. For example:

Michael said, "I sure am hungry."
Duane says, "I love to eat Italian food."

When an attribution is in the middle of a quotation, attach the attribution to whatever comes before it. Then, follow the attribution with a comma and treat it and the quotation that follows as if the attribution were before the quotation. For example:

"I love that idea!" *said Amber.* "This will be so much fun."
"I'm not sure," *commented Chase,* "if it will work."

When an attribution is placed at the end of the quotation and the quotation ends with a period, replace the period with a comma and follow the comma with the closing quotation mark. Then, write the attribution. For example:

"We can figure this out," *Pam said.*
"I'm happy with whatever everybody else wants," *Kelly stated.*

However, when a quotation ends with an exclamation point or a question mark, those punctuation marks must be retained. Don't replace them with commas. For example:

"Can I hang out with you guys?" *Bo asks.*
"Yes you can!" *Sondra answers.*

In dialog, you should always begin a new paragraph whenever a new speaker begins to talk. You should never have two or more speakers speak one after the other in a single paragraph. For example:

"Should I grow a mustache?" asked Gary.
Mary answered, "I don't think that would be such a great idea."

It is not always necessary to attribute each statement in dialog. If two people are talking, once you have told your audience who the two speakers are, and once they begin talking back and forth, the change of paragraph alone can serve to indicate that the speakers have changed. For example:

"Sam the ram can pass Val the nag," said Matt.
"Oh, sure!" said Jen.
"He can! He can! I'll prove it to you."
"Oh, yeah? How?"

Many authors attribute quotations with the simple word *said*. There is nothing wrong with using *said*. When writing dialog, you want people to focus more on the words that the characters are saying than the attributions. But if you use *said* in every paragraph, readers can become bored. To make your writing more interesting, try to use more interesting words in your attribution. For example:

> Joe Felder *asked*, "What are you doing?"
> Julian *replied*, "Nothing."

In A Nutshell:

Quotations are pieces of speech or writing repeated or copied exactly as spoken or written.

Quotation marks (" ") are marks of punctuation used to indicate exactly what someone else said or wrote.

The **attribution** is the phrase that indicates who said whatever it is you're quoting.

Application:

Choose several activities to do over the course of the week to reinforce what you've taught your children about quotations, quotation marks, and attributions:

☐ Review any of the songs we've covered already on your *Grammar Rock* DVD.

☐ Try to combine your history and grammar lessons this week. As you and your children study history together, use your books or the Internet to find some **Famous Quotes** from the people you're studying. Discuss the quotations and why they're famous. Then have your children write the quotations in a sentence. Make sure they use attributions and punctuate the sentences correctly.

☐ Have some fun playing a game of **Newspaper Reporter.** Your children will pretend to be a reporter from your local newspaper. You are a witness of some kind. You can be a policeman, a fireman, a shop owner … whoever you want to be! Just make sure that you've seen or heard something very interesting. Have your children interview you to discover what you know. Then have them write a few short paragraphs telling their readers all about it. Make sure they use good, exact quotations and correct punctuation in their written story. If you have time, have them think up a headline for their story and then "print" it to show to others.

☐ Play **Says Who?** on **Side A** of the **Lesson 29: Quotations** Student **Activity Sheet**. Have your children look over the chart on the activity sheet. The left side contains the names of several famous people. On the right side are some things that these people might have said (but probably didn't!). Ask your children to match the person with the quotation they believe he or she might have uttered at some point in time, and then have them write out the quotation in a new sentence with an attribution.

☐ Help your children **Fill in the Blank** on **Side B** of the <u>**Lesson 29:**</u> <u>**Quotations**</u> **Student Activity Sheet**. Ask your children what is wrong with the quotations on the activity sheet. If they guess they're all missing attributions, they're right. Have them read each quotation and fill in the blank with the attribution that they believe best fits the quotation.

Answer Key

Side A: Says Who?

Answers will vary.

Side B: Fill in the Blank

Answers will vary.

1. Abraham Lincoln: "I hate going to the theatre."
2. Napoleon Bonaparte: "My country will one day be world famous for these crispy fried potatoes!"
3. Paul Revere: "Hey! Here come a bunch of guys with guns!"
4. Cleopatra: "I'm not falling for another one of your pyramid schemes."

Lesson 30: Compounds

> COMPOUND: Compound refers to something composed of two or more parts, elements, or ingredients.

Teaching Instruction:

There are many compounds to deal with in grammar. We've already looked at compound sentences and compound-complex sentences. In this lesson, we'll learn about compound words, compound subjects, and compound predicates.

A **compound word** is a word made up of two or more smaller words. For example:

campground (camp/ground)
pillbox (pill/box)

A **compound subject** is made up of two or more simple subjects. The compound subject and its predicate(s), together, still form only one clause. For example:

Ryan and *Bo* love Japanese food.
Michael, Duane, and *Kelly* prefer German food.

A **compound predicate** is made up of two or more simple predicates applied to a single subject. The subject and the compound predicate, together, still form only one clause. For example:

Sondra's favorite restaurant *caught on fire* and *burned to the ground.*
The dog with only three legs *jumped through the ring of fire and rolled onto his side.*

In the first example, the simple predicates *caught on fire* and *burned to the ground* tell what happened to the single *subject* restaurant. In the second example, the simple predicates *jumped through the ring of fire* and *rolled onto his side* describe what the single subject *dog* did.

If your children are wondering why they're learning about compounds, you can explain to them that using compounds can improve their writing. Instead of writing two or more similar sentences, which can seem repetitive and boring, they can use compounds (words, subjects, or predicates) to simplify and clarify their writing. For example:

John ate bananas for breakfast.
John's monkey ate bananas for breakfast.
John drank orange juice for breakfast.
John's monkey drank orange juice for breakfast.
John and his monkey ate bananas and drank orange juice for breakfast.

Do you see how the use of compounds in the second example results in a clear, concise sentence that delivers the same information as the four sentences in the first example?

Notes:

Notes:

In A Nutshell:

A **compound word** is a word made up of two or more smaller words.

A **compound subject** is made up of two or more simple subjects.

A **compound predicate** is made up of two or more simple predicates applied to a single subject.

Application:

Choose several activities to do over the course of the week to reinforce what you've taught your children about compound words, compound subjects, and compound predicates:

☐ Review *A Noun is A Person Place Or Thing*, *Verb: That's What's Happening*, *The Tale Of Mr. Morton*, and *Conjunction Junction* on your *Grammar Rock* DVD.

☐ Encourage your children to so some more **Editing** of their recent work. Can they find any sentences that could be simplified or clarified by using compound words, compound subjects, or compound predicates? Challenge them to try to incorporate compounds and vary their sentence structure to make their writing more interesting.

☐ How many **Compound Words** can your children make from the words in the chart on **Side A** of the <u>Lesson 30: Compounds</u> **Student Activity Sheet**? Have them read through all of the words in the chart and then test their skill at combining them into compound words. Ask them to write as many new compound words as they can on the lines below the chart.

☐ Challenge your children to **Simplify and Clarify** the sentences on **Side B** of the <u>Lesson 30: Compounds</u> **Student Activity Sheet**. Sometimes we write in a way that's too confusing or unnecessarily repetitive. Ask your children to take a look at the groups of sentences listed on the Activity Sheet. Have them read each set and then try to rewrite them using compound subjects and/or compound predicates to make them simpler and clearer.

Answer Key

Side A: Compound Words

Answers will vary.

Side B: Simplify and Clarify

1. Fay and Sally love to play.
2. Amber closed the door, sat down, and cried.
3. Randy and Joe chased the beaver and jumped over the dam.
4. Duane, Melinda, and Oswald love to eat Italian food at Luigi's Restaurant.

Lesson 31: Contractions

> CONTRACTION: A contraction is a shortened form of a word or group of words, with the omitted letters often replaced by an apostrophe.

Teaching Instruction:

A **contraction** is a shortened version of a common word combination. The word contract means to squeeze together and make smaller. Thus, a contraction is a word made of two words that are put together and then made shorter.

When writing a contraction, leave no space between the words and use an apostrophe in place of the missing letters. Here are some examples of contractions:

do not → *don't*
should have → *should've*
it is → *it's*

In A Nutshell:

Contractions are shortened versions of common word combinations.

Just for Fun!

Homographs are words that are spelled alike but have different meanings. Homographs may or may not sound alike. For example:

bow (on a package)
bow (to shoot an arrow)
bow (what a violinist uses)
bow (the front part of a boat)
bow (what a violinist does when the audience claps)

Homonyms are words that sound the same but do not mean the same thing. Homonyms may be spelled the same, or they may be spelled differently. For example:

be/bee
deer/dear
piece/peace

Homonyms that are spelled exactly the same as another word are homographs also. For example, the words bow (on a package) and bow (to shoot an arrow) are homonyms and homographs. The words time and thyme are homonyms but, obviously, not homographs: they are not spelled the same, they do not mean the same thing, and they are spelled differently. All homographs that sound the same are homonyms, but not all homonyms are homographs.

Notes:

Application:

Choose several activities to do over the course of the week to reinforce what you've taught your children about contractions:

☐ Review any of the songs we've covered already on your **Grammar Rock DVD**.

☐ Play a game of **Contraction Memory**. Make a set of 3"x5" index cards with various words that are often part of contractions, such as I, he, she, we, you, is, could, would, not, have, are, am, etc. Then lay out the cards face down on a table. Take turns choosing a pair of cards. If the cards chosen can be made into a contraction (*I* and *am*, for example, can make *I'm*), you keep the pair and score points. If the words can't be made into a contraction (*I* and *we*, for example), then turn the cards back over. A good memory will help you remember where certain words are and score more contraction pairs.

☐ Ask your children to **Expand** the contractions on **Side A** of the <u>**Lesson 31: Contractions**</u> **Student Activity Sheet**. We have listed several contractions. Can your children expand them back into the separate words from which they're formed? Have them write the expanded forms on the lines provided.

☐ Challenge your children to **Contract** the words listed on **Side B** of the <u>**Lesson 31: Contractions**</u> **Student Activity Sheet**. We have listed several pairs of words. Can your children put them together to form a contraction? Make sure they don't forget the apostrophes! Have them write the contractions on the lines provided.

Answer Key

Side A: Expand

1. is not
2. will not
3. he will
4. had not
5. would have
6. I am
7. we will
8. she is
9. they are
10. does not
11. you will
12. they have
13. she will
14. I have
15. are not
16. that is

Side B: Contract

1. won't
2. he'll
3. you've
4. don't
5. that's
6. they'll
7. she's
8. they're
9. it's
10. weren't
11. she's
12. let's
13. it'll
14. hasn't
15. shouldn't
16. I'm

Lesson 32: More Nouns

> **N**OUN: A noun is the part of speech that names people, places, things, or ideas. Nouns come in three forms. Proper nouns are names; common nouns are the general kinds of things that proper nouns name; pronouns are used in place of proper and common nouns.

Teaching Instruction:

Notes:

In this lesson, we're going to take a closer look at two special types of nouns: nouns of direct address and possessive nouns.

A **noun of direct address** identifies to whom one is speaking. For example:

> "Doug, please pass the pear butter."

Always use commas to set off nouns of direct address from the rest of the sentence in which they appear. If the noun of direct address comes at the beginning of the sentence, put the comma after it. If it's in the middle of the sentence, put commas before and after it. If it's at the end of the sentence, put the comma before it.

> "*Mom*, do I have to?"
> "Of course, *Karleen*, you know you have to."
> "Would you like fries with that, *Mr. Ballard*?"

Possessive nouns are used to show ownership. A possessive noun will end with an apostrophe-s ('s) or s-apostrophe (s'). For example:

> *Matt and Jean's* pig (the pig belongs to Matt and Jean)
> *Ms. Andersen's* armadillo (the armadillo belongs to Ms. Andersen)
> The *books'* covers (the covers are owned by more than one book)

There are various rules governing the proper use of possessive nouns. For singular nouns, add apostrophe-s ('s) to the end to make it possessive. For example:

> chair
> chair + 's = chair's
> That chair's leg is broken.

For plural nouns not ending in s, add apostrophe-s ('s) to the end to make it possessive. For example:

> children
> children + 's = children's
> The children's play was held before the holidays.

For plural nouns ending with s, add only the apostrophe (') to the end to make it possessive. For example:

> books
> books + ' = books'
> All of the books' covers were torn.

For singular nouns ending in s, you can add apostrophe-s ('s) or only the apostrophe (') to make it possessive. For example:

> Jesus: Jesus + ' = Jesus' **or** Jesus + 's = Jesus's
> Jesus' light shines for all of us to see. **or** Jesus's light shines
>   for all of us to see.

Note: The shorter version (only the apostrophe) is usually preferred, especially if the ending "iz" sound is not wanted.

Notes:

Possessive nouns can be tricky. You can no longer rely solely on the pronunciation of a word for its meaning. In the following examples, *chipmunks* is pronounced the same in each example, yet these examples reveal four distinct meanings:

> The chipmunks are playing. (more than one chipmunk is playing)
> The chipmunk's asleep. (one chipmunk is asleep)
> The squirrel is eating the chipmunk's food. (the food belongs to the chipmunk)
> I found the chipmunks' house. (the house belongs to the chipmunks)

When more than one person in a series owns something, only attach the apostrophe-s ('s) to the last person. For example:

> Randy and Tim's aardvark ran away. (the aardvark is owned by both of them)
> Randy's and Tim's aardvarks love to play together. (each owns his own aardvark)

In A Nutshell:

A **noun of direct address** identifies to whom one is speaking.

Possessive nouns are used to show ownership. A possessive noun will end with an apostrophe-s ('s) or s-apostrophe (s').

Application:

Choose several activities to do over the course of the week to reinforce what you've taught your children about nouns of direct address and possessive nouns:

☐ Review *A Noun is A Person Place Or Thing* and *Rufus Xavier Sarsaparilla* on your *Grammar Rock* DVD.

☐ Help your children practice possessive nouns by challenging them to **Convert** possessive pronouns in their reading back into possessive nouns. For example, as you're reading together, you will come across a variety of possessive pronouns: mine, theirs, his, hers, theirs, its, etc. When you see these words, ask your children to convert them back into a regular possessive nouns: John's, Joan's, the kids', Fred and Ethel's, the cat's, etc.

☐ We have a question: **"Children, Where Do The Commas Go?"** Can your children tell us on **Side A** of the **Lesson 32: More Nouns Student Activity Sheet**? All of the sentences on the Activity Sheet contain nouns of direct address. However, when we wrote them, we forgot to put in the commas. Can your children help us out? Have them read through the sentences and fill in the missing commas where they belong.

☐ Help! There are **Missing Apostrophes** on **Side B** of the **Lesson 32: More Nouns Student Activity Sheet**. We found a bunch of sentences with possessive nouns in the back of the closet. Unfortunately, all of the apostrophes were missing. We suspect they may have gotten stuck in a coat pocket or fallen into a pair of boots. In any case, they're missing and we need your children's help. Have them read through the sentences on the Activity Sheet and put the apostrophes back into the sentences where they belong. Hint: We've given all the clues your children will need to place them in the appropriate places.

Answer Key

Side A: Children, Where Do The Commas Go?

1   Yes, Martha, the pigeons will fly away if you clap your hands.
2. John, what time do you want to go to the movies?
3. Don't forget to renew your library book, Gary.
4. Max, don't antagonize the llama.
5. Pick up the pieces, Loretta, and put them back together.
6. Please pass the parmesan cheese, Cindy.
7. Is that your phone ringing, Mr. Jenkins?
8. Todd, throw the baseball to the third baseman next time.
9. If you open the door, Mitch, I'll give you a surprise.
10. Jean, did you break your wrist when you fell?
11. That's the best frosting I've ever eaten, Stephanie!
12. When the flag drops, Andy, press the accelerator as hard as you can.

Side B: Missing Apostrophes

1. I will not sit on that chair. One of the chair's legs is broken.
2. Jason and Jennifer have three children. Their children's favorite-holiday is Christmas.
3. Jolie owns two badgers. Max owns three badgers. Jolie's and Max's badgers' sharp teeth help them eat tough foods.
4. Donald keeps one duck at home under his bed. Donald's duck's quack wakes him up when it's time to get up to go to school.
5. The motorcycles' roaring engines scared the geese grazing by the pond.
6. Twelve elves' teeth chattered as they waited for the big guy to return home.

Lesson 33: Restrictive & Nonrestrictive Clauses & Phrases

> **R**ESTRICTIVE CLAUSE OR PHRASE: A restrictive clause or phrase limits the meaning of a modified element.
>
> **N**ONRESTRICTIVE CLAUSE OR PHRASE: A nonrestrictive clause or phrase describes a modified element rather than limiting the element's meaning.

Teaching Instruction:

A **restrictive clause or phrase** adds information that is essential to the meaning of a sentence. You should not set off a restrictive clause or phrase with commas, parentheses, dashes, or any other punctuation that might set it apart from the rest of the sentence. For example:

> Customers with strollers may not use the escalator.

If you remove the phrase *with strollers*, the meaning of the sentence would change. The phrase *with strollers* restricts the meaning of the sentence: only those customers *with strollers* may not use the escalator. Here's another example:

> You can't get there from here.

The meaning of this sentence changes if you remove the restrictive phrase *from here*. Without the restrictive phrase *from here*, the sentence would mean you can't get there at all!

NOTE: Some appositives, which would normally be set off with commas, are restrictive. They narrow or focus the meaning of the noun they are renaming or describing. These restrictive appositives should not be set off with commas. For example:

> I think his ferret Hildegard is spoiled.
> My favorite is the author Robert Ludlum.

A **nonrestrictive clause or phrase** adds information that is interesting but not essential to the meaning of a sentence. You can tell that a clause is nonrestrictive if the meaning of the sentence does not change when you remove it. When you include a nonrestrictive clause or phrase, surround it by commas. For example:

> I smiled, resting a weary arm on my friend's shoulder.

The phrase *resting a weary arm on my friend's shoulder* certainly adds information, but it is not essential to understanding the message of the sentence: I smiled. Removing this nonrestrictive phrase would not change the meaning of the sentence. Here's another example:

> Even though my house is small, I can't hear the kids when they
> are in the basement.

The clause *Even though my house is small* makes the sentence more interesting, but its removal does not affect the meaning of the sentence: *I can't hear the kids when they are in the basement.*

NOTE: The words *that* and *which* often cause confusion amongst students trying to learn their proper usage. *That* should be used at the beginning of restrictive clauses (no commas!), while *which* should be used at the beginning of nonrestrictive clauses (preceded by a comma). For example:

> The ape that attacked the zookeeper was caught yesterday.
> The ape, which many people find repulsive, dwells in the jungle.

Notes:

Notes:

In A Nutshell:

Restrictive clauses or phrases add information that is essential to the meaning of a sentence. Don't use commas!

Nonrestrictive clauses or phrases add information that is interesting but not essential to the meaning of a sentence. Use commas!

Just for Fun!

An **interjection** is a one- or two-word expression of emotion that doesn't communicate significant meaning. It usually ends with an exclamation point, or it can be set off from the rest of a sentence with commas. For example:

"*Oh*, I wish I could go on vacation."
"*Wow!* Do you really have a turkey?"

Application:

Choose several activities to do over the course of the week to reinforce what you've taught your children about restrictive and nonrestrictive clauses or phrases:

☐ Review any or all of the songs on your ***Grammar Rock*** DVD that we've covered thus far.

☐ Challenge your children to become **Article Sleuths**. Provide them with a variety of newspaper and/or magazine articles to search, then challenge them to find twenty (or more) clauses or phrases of each type (restrictive and nonrestrictive).

☐ After your children have found a variety of restrictive and nonrestrictive clauses or phrases in the articles you provided, ask them to play **Editor-In-Chief**. Can they turn the restrictive clauses and phrases into nonrestrictive ones? And vice versa? This exercise, while not easy, will help them to think creatively about sentence structure and how it is possible to word (and re-word) sentences to convey the same meaning in various ways.

☐ The chart on **Side A** of the <u>**Lesson 33: Restrictive & Nonrestrictive Clauses & Phrases**</u> **Student Activity Sheet** contains several sentences with either restrictive or nonrestrictive clauses or phrases. Can your children figure out **Which Is It?** Ask them to read each sentence to determine what type of clause or phrase it features, then put an "X" in the appropriate column to the right.

☐ It's time for your children to put what they've learned about restrictive and nonrestrictive clauses into action by doing some **(Almost) Free Writing**. On the lines on **Side B** of the <u>**Lesson 33: Restrictive & Nonrestrictive Clauses & Phrases**</u> **Student Activity Sheet**, ask your children to write two sentences with a restrictive clause or phrase and two sentences with a nonrestrictive clause or phrase, using the clauses or phrases contained in the chart on the Activity Sheet.

Answer Key

Side A: Which Is It?

1. Restrictive
2. Nonrestrictive
3. Nonrestrictive
4. Restrictive
5. Nonrestrictive
6. Restrictive
7. Restrictive
8. Restrictive
9. Nonrestrictive

Side B: (Almost) Free Writing

Answers will vary.

Notes:

Lesson 34: More Pronouns

> **P**RONOUN: Pronouns are words that are used as substitutes for nouns and whose referents are named or understood from the surrounding context.

Teaching Instruction:

In this lesson, we will delve more deeply into the world of pronouns. Not only will we look at some more advanced aspects of pronouns in general, we will look closer at some specific special types of pronouns. Remember: Mastery of all of these concepts is not necessary now. Strive for a general, broad understanding at this point.

Each personal pronoun has three **cases**:

1. **Nominative**—when the pronoun is the subject of a sentence (I, we, you, he, she, it, they)

2. **Objective**—when the pronoun is the object of the sentence (me, us, you, him, her, it, them)

3. **Possessive**—when the pronoun owns something (my, mine, our, your, his, her, its, their)

The table below shows the correct pronouns to use depending on the case, person, and number of the noun:

Pronouns			
Person/Number:	Nominative:	Possessive:	Objective:
1st/Singular	I went to bed.	That is my bed.	That hurt me.
1st/Plural	We went to bed.	Those are our beds.	That hurt us.
2nd/Singular	You went to bed.	That is your bed.	That hurt you.
2nd/Plural	You went to bed.	Those are your beds.	That hurt you.
3rd/Singular Masculine	He went to bed.	That is his bed.	That hurt him.
3rd/Singular Feminine	She went to bed.	That is her bed.	That hurt her.
3rd/Singular Neutral	It went to bed.	That is its bed.	That hurt it.
3rd/Plural	They went to bed.	Those are their beds.	That hurt them.

NOTE: Except in the case of the neutral person, you cannot substitute the first and third person nominative and objective cases. For example:

Correct:	Incorrect:
"My mom gave me a dollar."	"My mom gave I a dollar."

Notes:

An **intensive pronoun** is a pronoun with the suffix *-self* or *-selves*. An intensive pronoun intensifies or emphasizes the noun or pronoun to which it refers. For example:

Sondra picked the restaurant all by *herself*.

Intensive pronouns serve only to add emphasis to (to intensify) a noun or pronoun already in the sentence. In the example above, the pronoun *herself* serves to emphasize that Sondra picked the restaurant on her own.

Reflexive pronouns also have a *-self* or *–selves* suffix. Reflexive pronouns are used as the object of a sentence when referring back to the subject of the sentence. For example:

Randy hurt himself.

Reflexive pronouns will always be (1) direct objects that are (2) the same as the subject. In the example above, the pronoun *himself* is the direct object of the verb *hurt* and it reflects back to Randy, the subject of the sentence.

NOTE: Compound personal pronouns function as either reflexive or intensive pronouns and include myself, yourself, himself, herself, and itself (singular) and ourselves, yourselves, and themselves (plural).

Interrogative pronouns are pronouns that are used only when asking a question. They include who, which, and what. For example:

Who are you? *Which* is the shortest route? *What* do you want?

Interrogative pronouns can function as either a subject or as an object of a verb or a preposition. For example, the interrogative pronoun who has three forms, depending upon how it is used in a sentence:

subject form:	*who*
object form:	*whom*
possessive form:	*whose*

Just to make things difficult, *who* (and its other forms, *whose* and *whom*), *which*, and *what* (along with the demonstrative pronoun *that*) can also be relative pronouns. **Relative pronouns** connect (relate) phrases or clauses to nouns or other pronouns. The most common relative pronouns are who, whoever, which, and that. For example:

The anteater *who* runs the fastest usually wins the race.

So how do you know whether these pronouns are interrogative or relative when you find them in a sentence? It depends upon how they're being used in the sentence. If they're used when asking a question, they're interrogative pronouns. On the other hand, if they introduce a clause and relate that clause back to their antecedents, then they're relative pronouns. For example:

Who is the boy with the trophy? (interrogative)
Seth is the boy *who* won the soccer championship. (relative)

NOTE: Compound relative pronouns are used in the same way. These include: whatever, whatsoever, whichever, whoever, whomever, whomsoever, whosesoever, and whosoever.

Indefinite pronouns are pronouns that refer to nothing in particular. For example:

> *Everybody* was excited about the big anteater race.

Here is a list of the most common indefinite pronouns: all, any, anybody, anyone, anything, both, each, each one, each other, either, everybody, everyone, everything, few, many, neither, nobody, none, no one, nothing, one, one another, ones, other, others, several, some, somebody, someone, and something.

Demonstrative pronouns identify specific persons, places, or things. They include this and that (singular) and these and those (plural). For example:

> *This* is fantastic!
> I'm not so sure about *that*.

Be careful, though! These same words can be used as adjectives. If they're used in place of nouns, they're demonstrative pronouns. For example:

> *That* is my ball.

If they're used with nouns, however, they're **demonstrative adjectives**. For example:

> *That* ball is mine.

A **possessive pronoun** is a special form of pronoun that shows possession. To make a possessive pronoun, do not add an apostrophe-s ('s) or an s-apostrophe (s') to the root pronoun. Instead, use a special form of the pronoun. For example:

> If I own something, it is *my* thing, or *mine*.
> If we own something, it is *our* thing, or *ours*.
> If you own something, it is *your* thing, or *yours*.
> If he owns something, it is *his* thing.
> If she owns something, it is *her* thing, or *hers*.
> If it owns something, it is *its* thing.
> If they own something, it is *their* thing, or *theirs*.

Possessive pronouns can be used alone (The basketball is *his*.) or to modify a noun (We played with *his* basketball.).

NOTE: Never use apostrophes with any possessive pronoun.

In A Nutshell:

Nominative case—when the pronoun is the subject of a sentence

Objective case—when the pronoun is the object of the sentence

Possessive case—when the pronoun owns something

An **intensive pronoun** is a pronoun with the suffix -self or -selves that intensifies or emphasizes the noun or pronoun to which it refers.

Reflexive pronouns also have a -self or –selves suffix and are used as the object of a sentence when referring back to the subject.

Interrogative pronouns are pronouns that are used only when asking a question.

Relative pronouns connect phrases or clauses to nouns or other pronouns.

Indefinite pronouns are pronouns that refer to nothing in particular.

Demonstrative pronouns identify specific things.

A **possessive pronoun** is a special form of pronoun that shows possession.

Application:

Choose several activities to do over the course of the week to reinforce what you've taught your children about the many different types of pronouns covered in this lesson:

☐ Review *Rufus Xavier Sarsaparilla* on your *Grammar Rock* DVD. If you want, review *A Noun is A Person Place Or Thing* as well.

☐ Give your children an assortment of newspaper or magazine articles and tell them to be a **Pronoun Pirate**. The treasure they're in search of is a pile of pronouns. More specifically, challenge them to find the types of pronouns we covered in this lesson: intensive, reflexive, interrogative, relative, indefinite, demonstrative, and possessive pronouns.

☐ Remember the **A Penny For A Pronoun** game from Lesson 7? Play it again this week (if you have any change left!). To refresh your memory: You need to get a bag full of pennies and keep it in your pocket. Explain to your children that you will give them a penny every time you use a pronoun and they catch you. Purposefully try to use more common and proper nouns rather than pronouns. Even refer to yourself in the third person for fun (for example, "Judy loves ice cream" rather than "I love ice cream"). Try to use the specific types of pronouns we covered in this lesson, if possible.

☐ Challenge your children to **Fill in the Blank** on **Side A** of the **Lesson 34: More Pronouns** **Student Activity Sheet**. We're having some trouble with our pronouns. Can your children help us out? Ask them to read the sentences on the Activity Sheet and insert the appropriate pronouns in the blanks.

☐ We want your children to write **9 Sentences** on **Side B** of the **Lesson 34: More Pronouns** **Student Activity Sheet**. We want them to be their absolute craziest, most creative selves today. Encourage them to delve deeply into the inner recesses of their wildest imaginations and create 9 sentences featuring the types of pronouns we covered in this lesson. Ask them to use the lines on the Activity Sheet to write sentences containing the types of pronouns indicated.

Answer Key

Side A: Fill in the Blank

1. I
2. me
3. their
4. herself
5. Everyone
6. who
7. That, mine
8. herself, She
9. I, me
10. I, I, myself

Side B: 9 Sentences

Answers will vary.

Lesson 35: More Verbs

> **V**ERB: Verbs are words that express actions, occurrences, or modes of being. Verbs form the predicate of a sentence and can be inflected for agreement with the subject, for tense, for voice, for mood, or for aspect.

Teaching Instruction:

In this lesson, we will explore the many specific types of verbs. Remember: Mastery of all of these concepts is not necessary now. Strive for a general, broad understanding at this point.

Helping (or auxiliary) verbs modify the meaning of primary verbs. They can control verb tenses and express a sense of necessity, certainty, probability, or possibility. For example:

> Seth *had* gone.
> Herman *will* go.
> Maggie *was* going.
> That *might have* meant a lot of trouble for her.

Intransitive verbs have no direct objects. They do not transfer any action from one noun to another. Intransitive verbs talk about actions that affect no one and nothing other than the subject itself. For example:

> Fran *slept*.
> John *jumped*.

You would never ask, "*What* did Fran sleep?" or "*Who* did she sleep?" Fran did the sleeping, and the sleeping affected Fran herself. Likewise, you don't need to ask, "*What* did John jump?" John did the jumping.

Transitive verbs require two nouns: (1) a subject to do the action; and (2) an object to receive the action or to be acted upon. Transitive verbs transfer action from one noun to another. For example:

> Noah *pushed* the zebras into the ark.

The verb *pushed* requires the subject *(Noah)* and an object *(the zebras)* to make sense. If the object is missing from the sentence, it will seem incomplete. For example:

> Alice *held*.
> Kenneth *broke*.

If someone told you that Alice held, you would want to know *what* Alice held. A cake? A rope? The bag? The transitive verb *held* requires a direct object. Likewise, you probably want to know what Kenneth broke. His leg? Your mom's fine china? You need to know *what* he broke.

A **linking verb** describes the way things *are* or *seem to be*. Linking verbs help identify connections between subjects and other nouns or adjectives. The nouns and adjectives to which linking verbs tie their subjects are called **predicate nouns** and **predicate adjectives**. For example:

> The water *seems* clear.
> Rutabagas *are* vegetables.

Notes:

In the first example above, *seems* is the linking verb and *clear* is the predicate adjective. In the second example, *are* is the linking verb and *vegetables* is the predicate noun.

There are also several linking verbs that suggest mere belief or sense that something is true (*feel, look, smell,* etc.) or that suggest the situation may be changing (*grow, become, stay,* etc.). Common linking verbs include the following: are, am, appear, stay, was, small, sound, look, were, seem, taste, turn, be, grow, feel, get, been, become, and remain.

Linking verbs are relatively weak verbs because they simply link; they don't *do* anything! Whenever possible, you should replace linking verbs with active verbs—verbs that actually do something. Sentences with active verbs are much more enjoyable to read.

Phrasal (or modal) verbs require another word—a helping verb, an infinitive, or a prepositional adverb—in order to make sense. For example:

> That coat *stands out*. —Coats don't stand. The preposition *out* is part of the phrasal verb *stand out*.
> They *get along* well together. —This sentence has no direct object for them to get. The preposition *along* is a part of the phrasal verb *get along*.
> The criminal was *picked up* by the police. —*Up* and *by* are both prepositions; but *up* does not indicate a direction. Here, the preposition up is a part of the phrasal verb *picked up*.

NOTE: Sometimes the direct object of a phrasal verb (the thing that the phrasal verb affects) may come between the base verb and the preposition. For example:

> *Hand over* the keys.
> or
> *Hand* them *over*.

In A Nutshell:

Helping (or auxiliary) verbs modify the meaning of primary verbs.

Intransitive verbs have no direct objects. They do not transfer any action from one noun to another.

Transitive verbs require two nouns: (1) a subject to do the action; and (2) an object to receive the action or to be acted upon.

A **linking verb** describes the way things *are* or *seem to be*. Linking verbs help identify connections between subjects and other nouns or adjectives.

Phrasal (or modal) verbs require another word—a helping verb, an infinitive, or a prepositional adverb—in order to make sense.

Just for Fun!

Abbreviations are shortened versions of commonly-used words. Normally, you indicate that you are using an abbreviation by putting a period after the abbreviation. For example:

> Mr. (for Mister)
> St. (for Street or Saint)
> Dr. (for Doctor or Drive)

An **acronym** is a special kind of abbreviation that does not need a period and is pronounced as one word. For example:

NASA (National Aeronautics and Space Administration)

An **initialism** is a special kind of abbreviation in which each letter used to form the abbreviation is pronounced separately. Like acronyms, initialisms do not need periods. For example:

FBI (Federal Bureau of Investigation)

Application:

Choose several activities to do over the course of the week to reinforce what you've taught your children about the many different types of verbs covered in this lesson:

☐ Review *Verb: That's What's Happening* on your *Grammar Rock* DVD.

☐ Have your children keep a **Verb Chart** this week. While they read alone or you read together, ask them to be on the lookout for the types of verbs we learned about in this lesson: helping (or auxiliary), transitive, intransitive, linking, and phrasal (or modal) verbs. As they identify these types of verbs, whave them write them in the chart below. Challenge them to find 10 of each type of verb. Give them a special prize when they complete the chart.

Helping	Transitive	Intransitive	Linking	Phrasal

☐ Challenge your children to do some **Editing** of their recent work. Have they been using too many boring linking verbs? Ask them to identify linking verbs in their writing assignments and try to eliminate them.

☐ Our sentences on **Side A** of the **Lesson 35: More Verbs Student Activity Sheet** are **Not Active Enough**. We seem to be using too many linking verbs lately. See! We just used one in that last sentence. We need to stop that. Ask your children to take a look at our sentences on the Activity Sheet. Can they identify the linking verbs and eliminate them? Have them rewrite the sentences without the linking verbs in a way that makes them more active. Encourage them to be creative with their new creations.

☐ Ask your children to complete the **Name That Verb** chart on **Side B** of the **Lesson 35: More Verbs** Student Activity Sheet. For each verb listed in the left column, have them identify whether it is a transitive verb or an intransitive verb, and then put an "x" in the appropriate column.

Answer Key

Side A: Not Active Enough

Answers will vary.

Side B: Name That Verb

1. Transitive
2. Intransitive
3. Transitive
4. Intransitive
5. Transitive
6. Intransitive
7. Intransitive
8. Transitive
9. Intransitive
10. Transitive

Lesson 36: Gerunds, Participles, & Infinitives

> **G**ERUND: A gerund is a verbal form that ends in -ing and functions as a noun.
> **P**ARTICIPLE: A participle is a verbal form used as an adjective.
> **I**NFINITIVE: An infinitive is a verbal form usually beginning with the word to that functions as a noun and names the action/state without specifying the subject.

Teaching Instruction:

Remember way back in Lesson 12 when we learned about active and passive voice? In this lesson, we're going to expand upon what we learned earlier about voice and take a closer look at gerunds, participles, and infinitives. If you need to, take a few minutes to review Lesson 12 before commencing with this lesson.

Verbals are good indicators of passive-voice sentences. Verbals are words derived from verbs that act as another part of speech. Verbals include gerunds, participles, and infinitives.

A **gerund** is a noun made from a verb. Gerunds end in –*ing*. For example:

> I love *singing*.
> *Playing* is fun.

Gerunds can take objects and be modified by adverbs, just like regular verbs. For example:

> *Climbing* stairs is a lot more difficult than *riding* an escalator.

The gerund *climbing* takes the object stairs, and the gerund *riding* takes the object escalator.

If you use a gerund in a sentence, you are writing in the passive voice. To make your sentences more active, get rid of gerunds whenever possible!

A **participle** is an adjective made from a verb. Participles usually end with the suffix –*ing* or -*ed*. Participles are sometimes called verbal adjectives. For example:

> Ryan fell into the *churning* water.
> Jay thinks that thunder is *terrifying*.

Participles can take objects and be modified by helping verbs and adverbs, just like regular verbs. For example:

> *Having hit* the sack at 10 o'clock, Pam was ready to milk the cows at dawn.

The participle *having hit* takes the object *sack* and modifies the proper noun *Pam*.

Participles are good indicators of passive-voice sentences. To get rid of the passive voice, try to eliminate participles whenever possible.

An **infinitive** is a verb form that functions as a noun, adverb, or adjective. Infinitives usually begin with the word *to*. For example:

> *To run* a marathon is his dream.
> Henrietta loves *to watch* movies at home on the couch.

Infinitives can take objects and be modified by adverbs, just like regular verbs. For example:

> *To climb* those stairs would about kill me.

The infinitive *to climb* takes the object *stairs*.

Notes:

Notes:

Some verbs almost always come together with infinitives. In fact, they don't make sense without infinitives. For example:

> She *has* to eat the pickle.
> I am *going* to buy a caramel latte.
> Adam *used* to go to the grocery store.

We usually think of the verbs that follow *used to, going to,* and *has to* as completely separate from the two words that precede them. But you should always interpret the verb that precedes the word *to* (*used, going, has,* etc.) as combining *with* the infinitive (*to go, to buy, to eat,* etc.) to form what is known as a **modal (or phrasal) verb**.

In A Nutshell:

A **gerund** is a noun made from a verb. Gerunds end in –*ing*.

A **participle** is an adjective made from a verb. Participles usually end with the suffix –*ing* or -*ed*.

An **infinitive** is a verb form that functions as a noun, adverb, or adjective. Infinitives usually begin with the word *to*.

Application:

Choose several activities to do over the course of the week to reinforce what you've taught your children about gerunds, participles, and infinitives:

☐ Review **Verb: That's What's Happening** or any of the other songs we've covered already on your **Grammar Rock** DVD.

☐ Repeat the **Voice Coach** activity from Lesson 12. Grab a few of your children's recent writing samples. Ask them to do another edit of them, trying to spot passive-voice sentences. How did they do? Are there many? Have they improved since Lesson 12? We hope so! Don't worry if they still find some passive-voice sentences, though. Writing in the active voice is a skill that takes lots of practice. Challenge your children to turn all of their passive-voice sentences into more interesting active-voice sentences.

☐ Remember the **Newspaper Editor** activity from Lesson 12? Do it again with your children this week. Ask them to be the editor and you pretend to be a rookie reporter. Find a few short newspaper articles from a local paper or online and submit them to your editor for review. In the role of editor, your children should carefully analyze the articles you've submitted for active- and passive-voice sentences. Ask them to point out passive-voice sentences they find. Challenge them to rewrite any passive-voice sentences they find in the active voice.

☐ We thought it would be fun to go back to when we first started writing to look at some of our early sentences. Oh boy, was that a mistake! Just look at the sentences on **Side A** of the <u>**Lesson 36: Gerunds, Participles, & Infinitives**</u> **Student Activity Sheet**. They're **Absolutely Awful**—awfully passive, if not just plain awful all the way around. Can your children help us? Ask them to identify the passive elements (gerunds, participles, and/or infinitives) and then eliminate them. Have them rewrite the sentences in a more active voice. If they can improve them in any other way, tell them to go for it!

☐ Think your children know the difference between gerunds, participles, and infinitives? Challenge them to prove it! The chart on **Side B** of the **Lesson 36: Gerunds, Participles, & Infinitives** **Student Activity Sheet** contains several sentences, each of which contains a gerund, a participle, or an infinitive. Ask your children to **Identify** which one each sentence contains and then put an "X" in the appropriate column to the right of the sentence.

Answer Key

Side A: Absolutely Awful

Answers will vary.

Side B: Identify

1. Infinitive
2. Gerund
3. Participle
4. Participle
5. Infinitive
6. Gerund
7. Infinitive
8. Gerund
9. Participle

Appendix: Advanced Grammar Concepts

Introductory Note

After you have finished the 36 lessons in The Grammar Ace, feel free to read through this appendix to learn more about the advanced grammar concepts covered herein. You shouldn't feel like you have to cover these concepts, though, to have a solid grammar foundation. The concepts discussed in this appendix are truly advanced concepts that are above and beyond the normal scope of basic grammar.

We have provided this appendix merely as a resource for you to use and rely upon should you have a question about an advanced concept that was not addressed in the 36 lessons that comprise the main body of the program.

This appendix will give you a quick definition and example for each advanced grammar concept. For some of the concepts, we include even more instruction to help you gain greater understanding (under the heading **TELL ME MORE!**). We hope this appendix will serve as a valuable resource for you.

Apostrophe

An apostrophe (') is a punctuation mark that can show possession, make contractions, or show when letters are left out. Apostrophes are also used to make letters, numbers, and signs plural.

Ex. the kids' cookbook (the cookbook belongs to the kids)

didn't (did not)

I'm waitin' for him. (shortened version of *waiting*)

Z's, 9's, $'s

Brackets

Brackets ([ ]) are marks of punctuation used within quoted material to set off additional and/or clarifying information or to indicate editorial corrections.

Ex. "She [the author's wife] is my greatest source of support."

"I'd like to buy twenty-seven [baseballs] before the start of the season."

Brackets may also be substituted for parentheses within parentheses for added clarity.

Ex. The fish tank (which is 39 gallons [the largest the store carries, of course] and very large) needs to be cleaned soon.

Cleft Sentence

A cleft sentence is a complex sentence formed when an original declarative sentence is divided ("cleft") into two clauses—a main clause and a subordinate clause—for the purpose of emphasizing a particular part of the sentence. Cleft sentences usually begin with either the word *there* or *it*, followed by some form of the verb *to be*.

Ex. Original sentence: Michael came up with the idea for the new lunch plan.
Cleft sentence: It was Michael who came up with the idea for the new lunch plan.

TELL ME MORE!
Cleft sentences have delayed subjects. In other words, the true subject of a cleft sentence is not *there* or *it*; the true subject—if there is one—is whatever noun follows the verb. See also *Subject*.

If *there* and *it* are not subjects, what are they? They are called expletives, because they simply fulfill a structural function within the sentence. See also *Expletive*.

Cleft sentences can also be created with what. Cleft sentences beginning with *what* will usually make an initial noun clause out of the primary verb of the sentence:

Ex. Your stubborn attitude caused this problem.

What caused this problem is your stubborn attitude.

Colon

The colon (:) is a punctuation mark with many functions. Using a colon is like saying, "I'm going to tell you something important: Now here it is." What follows the colon usually explains or expands upon what came before. We use also use colons to introduce clauses, quotations, and lists.

Ex. Emphasis: He knew what frightened him: sky diving.

Quotations: A whisper floated in the air: "Help me!"

Lists: Sarah has plenty of toys: dolls, a play-house, and a rocking horse.

Salutations: Dear President Bush: Time: 9:23pm

Chapter/Verse: Psalm 46:1 (also used to separate titles/subtitles and volumes/pages)

TELL ME MORE!
Colons should not come between verbs and their objects.

Ex.   I have: a dog, a horse, and a rhinoceros. (incorrect)

I have several animals: a dog, a horse, and a rhinoceros. (correct)

Correlative Conjunctions

Correlative conjunctions are conjunctions that work only in pairs.

Ex.   either/or (Maggie wants either the red one or the blue one.)

Neither/ nor (I have neither the money nor the time to invest in this!)

Dash

The dash (—) is a very useful punctuation mark that may best be described as a cross between a comma, a colon, and an ellipsis. The dash is sometimes known as the **em dash**. Here are a few examples of its many functions.

Ex.   To indicate a sudden break or change in the sentence. (At the end of her shift—and this was not all her fault—Sarah forgot to clock out.)

To set off an introductory series from its explanation. (A cake, a few close friends, a new turkey—these things made Ashley's birthday special.)

To set off parenthetical material that explains or clarifies a word or a phrase. (My favorite place—the grocery store at the end of the block—changed this neighborhood forever.)

To indicate interrupted speech in a dialog. (I cried, "What is—" "It's a turkey!" exclaimed Ashley.)

To emphasize a word, a series, a phrase, or a clause. (And then I turned around and saw who it was—the butler!)

Determiner

Determiners, like articles and quantifiers, serve as adjectives and always come immediately before the nouns they modify. Determiners, in particular, specify which specific thing (or things) you are talking about. If they are used by themselves, most determiners can also serve as demonstrative pronouns.

Ex.   *This* aardvark
That badger
These missiles
Those children
This is fantastic! (*This* is also a demonstrative pronoun in this sentence)
I'm not so sure about *that*. (*that* is also a demonstrative pronoun in this sentence)

Diagonal

A diagonal (/), or **slash**, is a mark of punctuation used to create fractions, show choices, or indicate line breaks in poetry.

Ex.   Although the recipe called for ½ cup flour, Margaret mistakenly put in 1½ cups.

To change channels, use the up/down button on the remote control.

Roses are red/ violets are blue/ I hope this example/ is helpful to you.

Ellipsis

An ellipsis (…) is a punctuation mark that looks like three periods in a row. Ellipses (plural for ellipsis) can indicate missing material, a pause, or an incomplete thought.

Ex.   To indicate in formal quotations that a portion of the quoted section has been left out. (Original: We the students of Andersen High School, in order to improve our education, do hereby protest. Quotation: "We the students … do hereby protest.")

To indicate a pause. (Ashley untied the bow and opened the box. Inside was a … could it be … yes, it was … a turkey!)

To indicate that a speaker didn't finish his sentence. (I just couldn't remember what I was going to …)

TELL ME MORE!

Ellipsis pauses are unlike comma, colon, and semicolon pauses, because they do not help the reader understand what the speaker is saying. They do help the reader know *how* the speaker is saying something, which can shed light on the speaker's meaning and character. Also, when used in quotations, they alert the reader to missing text, which is important to know for academic pursuits.

Ellipses can also indicate a pause: perhaps a speaker, gasping for breath, had to take a break from speaking; maybe he had to think deeply about exactly what word to use next, and so paused in mid-sentence before continuing…. Or maybe … the author … simply … wants … to slow … the reader … down. The ellipsis says, "Take note! Things … slow … down … here."

Ellipses at the end of sentences are always preceded by the closing punctuation of the sentence—a period, a question mark, or an exclamation point. It is for this reason that you find four "periods" in a row at the end of sentences. The first period is truly a period; the other three dots are simply parts of an ellipsis.

Expletive

An expletive is a word or phrase that conveys no independent meaning but merely fulfills a structural function within a sentence. Expletives usually take the form of the word *there* or *it*, followed by some form of the verb *to be*. They are commonly found at the beginning of cleft sentences. See also *Cleft Sentence*.

Ex. *It was* the papaya that fell off the kitchen table.
There were seven football players who got hurt.

Foreshadowing

Foreshadowing is a writing technique used to heighten the tension in a story. When using foreshadowing, an author will give hints or clues about what is going to happen later. Those hints and clues give you an inkling of what is to come … *before* it actually happens.

Ex. Michael was finishing his last long run of the week. As he turned the last corner toward home, he sensed that something was different. The cars parked along the street were not the usual ones he remembered seeing on previous trips down this block. (This paragraph gives the reader an inkling that something different is about to occur, probably involving the parked cars.)

Gerund Phrase

A gerund phrase consists of the gerund itself, plus any adverbs, objects, or other words whose meanings are directly tied to the gerund. A gerund phrase—like the gerund by itself—serves as a noun.

Ex. *Climbing stairs* is a lot more difficult than *riding an escalator.*

Hyphen

A hyphen is a punctuation mark with multiple uses. It looks like a short dash (-).

Ex. To divide words between their syllables when they are too long to fit on a single line

To join two or more words in compound numbers (*twenty-four, ninety-nine,* etc.)

To make compound words (*sixteen-year-old* boy)

To join single letters with other words (*T-shirt*)

To join numbers in scores, votes, life spans, etc. (*1865-1903, 24-17*)

To join two or more words that form a single adjective before a noun (*hard-working* man)

To prevent confusion (*re-create* instead of recreate)

Indentation

An indentation is an extra space that has been pushed in from the margin toward the middle of the page. Usually, the first line in a paragraph is indented.

Ex. Although Michael desperately wanted his computer fixed, Ryan decided that the problem was best ignored. Frustrated, but resigned, Michael continued his work. Unfortunately, the problem continued to rear its head. It would not be ignored!

Infinitive Phrase

An infinitive phrase consists of the infinitive itself plus any adverbs, objects, or other words whose meanings are directly tied to the infinitive itself. Like an infinitive, an infinitive phrase can serve as a noun, an adverb, or an adjective, but never as a verb.

Ex. *To climb those stairs* would about kill me.
I really don't want to *drive the car*.

Italics

Italics is a printing term that refers to type that is slightly slanted. In this sentence, the word *xylophone* is in italics. If you underline handwritten text it is normally set in *italics* when typeset. Italics are usually used for emphasis or ease of identification.

Ex. To identify titles of books, magazine titles, and album titles. (Michael is reading *The Design of Everyday Things*. Sondra has a subscription to *Bon Appetit*. MercyMe's song "I Can Only Imagine" is on the album *Almost There*.)

To add emphasis to a particular word or phrase. (No wonder you're lost! I told you to take the *right* turn in Albuquerque, not the left.)

To identify words being used. (The word *so* is a coordinating conjunction.)

To show that a word is in a foreign language. (Mix it all up and *voila*, you have a masterpiece.)

Margin

The margin is the space around the outside edges of a sheet of paper beyond the printed area.

Ex. This page you are reading has top, bottom, left, and right margins.

Meter

Meter is the "beat" of a piece of writing. Poetry, for example, can feature many different types of patterned repetition of stressed and unstressed syllables, giving poems a "feel" that often complements what their words express.

Ex. Many of Dr. Seuss' books feature delightful meter as a primary element.

Negative Statement

A negative statement expresses that something is not true. Negative statements usually feature words such as *no*, *not*, *nothing*, or *no one*.

Ex. I am *not* hot.
There is *nothing* to see here.
We have *no* more money.

TELL ME MORE!
No and not can also be adjectives or adverbs that modify nouns, adjectives, verbs, or other adverbs.

Ex. Modifying an adjective: That is *not* a cold duck. (Negating cold)

Modifying a noun: That is *not* a duck. (Negating duck)

Modifying a verb: He is *not* flying. (Negating flying)

Modifying an adverb: He's *not* flying high. (Negating high)

Non-vocalized Sounds

A non-vocalized sound is created when you say a word and/or create sound without using your vocal chords. You can tell if a sound is non-vocalized by placing your fingertips on your throat.

Ex. Say the /p/ or /k/ sound. You should feel no vibrations. Sometimes the suffix -ed is non-vocalized (it sounds like /t/—as in fixed).

Numerals

Numbers can either be spelled out (four, nine) or written as numerals (4, 9). There are many rules that govern when to use words and when to use numerals.

Ex. For numbers one to nine, use words; for numbers 10 & above, use numerals.

Use a combination for large numbers (7.9 trillion).

Maintain consistency if numbers are being compared or contrasted (four to ten or 4 to 10).

Use numerals for statistics, decimals, pages, chapters, and identifications (33%, 14.7, page 3, chapter 6, 555-1234, 14 Memory Lane, January 13, 1971, A.D. 36)

Use words for numbers at the start of a sentence (Twelve students are absent today).

For time and money, use numerals if abbreviations or symbols are used, but use words if spelled out (3:30 P.M., six o'clock, fifty dollars, $100).

Parentheses

Parentheses [( )] are marks of punctuation used to set off additional explanatory material that might otherwise disrupt regular sentence structure.

Ex.   Kaitlyn (my dog) loves to play in the snow.

Participial Phrase

A participial phrase consists of a participle plus any helping verbs, adverbs, objects, or other words whose meanings are directly tied to the participle. Participial phrases, like participles, serve as adjectives.

Ex.   *Eating her lunch*, Kelly discovered a worm in an apple. (the participle *eating* takes the direct object *lunch* and modifies the proper noun *Kelly*)

Having hit the sack at 10 o'clock, Pam was ready to milk the cows at dawn. (the participle *having hit* takes the object *sack* and modifies the proper noun *Pam*)

Quantifier

A quantifier is a special adjective that always comes immediately before the noun it modifies. Quantifiers tell us how many or how much of a thing we're talking about.

Ex.   *Twenty* bags of flour.
No papayas.
A *few* cordless screwdrivers.
All the bed bugs.

TELL ME MORE!
If they are used by themselves, most quantifiers can serve as pronouns.

Ex.   There are *none* left.
I own about *twenty*.
Hey! I said I wanted *two*!

Rhetorical Question

A rhetorical question is a question for which no answer is expected because the answer is so obvious or is simply not required.

Ex.   Are you kidding?
Can you believe it?

Semicolon

The semicolon (;) is a punctuation mark that acts like a weak period or a strong comma. The semicolon acts as a weak period when it replaces the period at the end of one sentence and stitches that sentence together with the next to form a single sentence. It acts as a strong comma by clearly showing the breaks between the members of a series (especially when one [or more] of the clauses or phrases in a series already contains commas).

Ex.   I did not call myself a musician; I told people that I played the guitar. (joining two or more independent clauses that are not connected with a coordinating conjunction)

I never forget to bring my beach gear when I go to the ocean—sun block, visor, and sunglasses; snorkel, fins, and water wings; towel, bathing suit, and flip flops. (separating groups of words that already contain commas)

Sentence Fragment

A sentence fragment is one or more words that do not form a complete thought punctuated as a sentence. It is not a complete sentence, because it is missing a subject, a predicate, or both. A sentence fragment may also be a subordinate clause.

Ex.   Penguins across the ice. (The sentence fragment is a missing a verb. Adding a verb will make it a complete sentence: Penguins *skated* across the ice.)

When the Zamboni was finished. (This sentence fragment is a subordinate clause. Adding an independent clause will make it a complete sentence: When the Zamboni was finished, *penguins skated across the ice*.)

Spinning and doing pirouettes. The penguins rocked the house. (The sentence fragment Spinning and doing pirouettes is followed by a complete sentence. The two can be joined to form one complete sentence: Spinning and doing pirouettes, the penguins rocked the house.)

Slang

Slang is the nonstandard vocabulary of a particular group or subculture, consisting usually of colorful figures of speech. Often used in fiction or personal writing, slang should be avoided in formal writing.

Ex. Phil needs to *seriously chill out*. (Phil really needs to relax.)

Michael couldn't believe his *homey* had *ratted him* out to the *fuzz*. (Michael couldn't believe his friend had turned him over to the police.)

Syllable/Syllabication Rule

A syllable is a small unit of speech made up of a single, uninterrupted sound. Words may have one or many syllables.

Ex. jump (one syllable—*jump*)
jumping (two syllables—*jump-ing*)
anesthesiologist (seven syllables—
an-es-the-si-ol-o-gist)

TELL ME MORE!

The main reason to study syllables is learn to break words when they need to be broken. Syllables are the smallest parts of words that you are allowed to print on one line. If you need to break a word, you should write all the syllables you can on the first line, place a hyphen at the end of the line, and then finish the word on the line that follows.

Ex. A common break point between syllables is between two consonants that are between two vowels (vc/cv—with v indicating vowels, c consonants). The syllables in the word picnic, for example, break between the consonants c and n, which are, in turn, between two vowels—i and i, respectively (pic/nic).

Vocalized Sounds

A vocalized sound is created when you say a word and/or create sound by using your vocal chords. You can tell if a sound is vocalized by placing your fingertips on your throat.

Ex. Say the /m/ sound. Can you feel the vibrations? Those indicate you are vocalizing. Sometimes the suffix -ed is vocalized (it sounds like /d/—as in played).